EXPLORING NONTRADITIONAL JOBS FOR WOMEN

By
Rose Neufeld

photographs by
William Neufeld

THE ROSEN PUBLISHING GROUP, Inc.
New York

Published in 1987, 1989 by The Rosen Publishing Group, Inc.
29 East 21st Street, New York, NY 10010

Copyright 1987, 1989 by Rose Neufeld

All rights reserved. No part of this book may be reproduced in any form without permission in writing from the publisher, except by a reviewer.

Revised Edition 1989

Library of Congress Cataloging-in-Publication Data

Neufeld, Rose.
  Exploring nontraditional jobs for women.

  (Careers in depth)
  Includes index.
  1. Vocational guidance for women—United States.
I. Title. II. Series.
HF5382.65.N48   1987   331.7′02′024042   86-29827
ISBN 0-8239-0971-9

Manufactured in the United States of America

Dedication

To the generous women herein, who willingly shared their experiences with all of us, this book is gratefully dedicated.

ROSE NEUFELD

WILLIAM NEUFELD

About the Author

Rose Neufeld, who has a master's degree in Vocational Guidance from New York University, was for many years a vocational guidance counselor in community agencies. She initiated programs designed to overcome problems in training and placement for job seekers with a variety of special handicaps.

For the past twenty years she has been teaching in secondary schools in the New York City school system. In addition to this book, she is the author of three other books for young people.

About the Photographer

William Neufeld is a photographer and filmmaker who has spent many years producing corporate and documentary work.

EXPLORING NONTRADITIONAL JOBS FOR WOMEN

MARYANN LANE, CARPENTER

Acknowledgments

The author wishes to acknowledge the help of the following people and organizations in the development of this book: John Bertollini, Bill Coke, Charles Flanders, Lillian Fuchs, Dixon Gross, Minna Hilton, Tom Moran, Jim Nolan, Bob Porgorzelski, Bill Speath, Brian Smith, Joan Stewart, Robert Van Zandt, Linette Viziani, Apex Technical School, Aviation Trades High School, Butler Aviation, The Caring Community, Cathedral of St. John the Divine, Channel 13, Chelsea Houses, Germaine School of Photography Division of Center for Media Arts, NABET, New Employment for Women, New Jersey Bell, New Jersey Transit Corp., New York City Technical College, New York Telephone Co., Prestin Spearin and Burro Construction Co., Public Service Electric and Gas Co., Sears Roebuck Corp., Technical Career Institute, Teterboro School of Aviation.

Contents

	Introduction	1
I.	Construction	5
	Carpenter	6
	Stonemason	11
	Glazier	16
	Painter	20
II.	Electric Power	26
	Cable Splicer	26
III.	Telephone	32
	Central Office Technician	32
	Line Installer	37
	Telephone Installer	43
IV.	Television	49
	Broadcast Technician	49
	Camera Operator	56
V.	Transportation	63
	Bus Driver	63
	Local Truck Driver	69
VI.	Mechanics, Repairers, and Related Occupations	76
	Air Conditioning, Refrigeration and Heating Mechanic	76
	Aircraft Mechanic	83
	Automobile Mechanic	89
	Boiler Tender	95
	Building Custodian	99
	Electronics Technician	105

	Locksmith	112
	Maintenance Electrician	118
VII.	Summary	125
VIII.	Writing Yourself Up	129
	Résumé	129
	Letter of Application	131
	"Thank You" Letter	132
IX.	The Twenty-first Century: Women's Workforce	133
	Appendix A. Federal Agencies	138
	Appendix B. State Apprenticeship Agencies	143
	Appendix C. Women's Organizations	147
	Index	151

Introduction

We know that you, today's young woman, face many challenges in your working life. These differ greatly from the problems women dealt with twenty years ago. In addition, the days of Cinderella are over, and you can no longer expect to be carried off by a handsome prince to live happily ever after, far from the world of work. Years ago, employment was simply a "filler" for the time between education and marriage. Most women expected to settle down to a life as wife and mother. When we examine our lives today, we realize this seldom happens. Among factors responsible for today's realities are the following:

- The divorce rate is up by 127 percent since 1960 and is rising.
- Only one out of five women in divided families receives child support.
- Women are remaining single longer and need to support themselves for a more extended time.
- Women are heads of household for one out of every seven families.
- Wives are joining husbands in working to make essential household contributions.
- Family size is decreasing.
- Only seven percent of families in our country represent the one-earner, husband-supported family.

Another dramatic change has been the trend for mothers with children, sometimes infants, to continue their employment. Many have returned to work after a brief maternity leave. This represents a substantial change from the days when women married and left jobs to raise their children. Perhaps years later, some might reenter the job market.

While women have made some important gains in the last ten years, with slowly increasing numbers in the professional and administrative occupations, the vast majority are still segregated in low-paying industries in clerical and service jobs. This concentration limits women's choices to a narrow range of low-status jobs. The most common of these traditional jobs are:

- secretary,
- typist,
- bookkeeper,
- cashier,
- registered nurse,
- waitress,
- nurse's aide,
- elementary school teacher,
- salesperson.

Since these jobs pay so poorly, it's not surprising that for every 64 cents earned by the average woman, the average man earns one dollar.

Although some women are able to become self-supporting in these traditional jobs, they experience frustration, boredom, lack of recognition, and lack of opportunity to move up the skill and career ladders. Therefore, since you are not only going to marry and raise children, but will probably also be employed, you should prepare for the eventuality of a lifetime in the working world.

You can widen your range of career choices, use your aptitudes and talents, and increase your earning power. One way to do this is to consider nontraditional jobs in the industrial "blue-collar" occupations.

By nontraditional we mean jobs in the skilled trades that have had large proportions of men workers and few, if any, women workers. These jobs are mainly in the construction trades, skilled crafts, and technical fields. Most do not require a college education, but do necessitate further training after high school. Apprenticeship is the most effective route into many of these higher-paying trades.

Apprentices are paid beginners who work on the actual job site under the supervision of skilled, experienced workers. Usually, apprentices attend evening school in job-related courses such as math, science, and technical subjects. This formal schooling is often sponsored and operated by a joint committee of the employers and the union. While learning, an apprentice receives a salary, which increases regularly. The formal apprenticeship lasts from two to four years. Jobs in the construction industry, such as electrician, carpenter, and glazier, have these apprenticeships.

A more informal type of training for nontraditional jobs also takes place on the job, but sometimes for months rather than years. Here, also, the apprentice learns by working as a helper or assistant to a skilled worker. This on-the-job training is sometimes supplemented by the employer's classroom instruction during the regular workday. The length of time for apprenticeship for these jobs varies from several weeks to a number of months. Jobs in this group are:

- telephone installer,
- cable splicer,
- locksmith.

Although there is urgent need for career options in nontraditional jobs for women, occupational sex stereotyping is a substantial problem. Certain jobs are still thought of as suitable only for men. Even though women in both World Wars worked at every kind of nontraditional job to keep industry going, myths still exist about women's mental and physical abilities. If you choose nontraditional work you may find resistance from those around you such as:

- parents,
- husbands, boyfriends,
- teachers,
- guidance counselors,
- women friends,
- co-workers.

Your friends or family may be embarrassed by your choice of a nontraditional occupation, believing that work as an auto mechanic, stonemason, or electronics technician is unfit or inappropriate for a woman. Harassment of women in vocational classes and on the job also remains as evidence of sex stereotyping and presents an obstacle in securing training and employment.

Another handicap for women considering nontraditional

occupations is the lack of early preparation. Girls are not encouraged in junior or senior high school to take shop, math, or science courses. Fathers don't encourage their daughters to help in making repairs at home. Therefore, girls don't become familiar with the use of simple mechanical tools. All of these barriers and prejudices ignore the evidence that women have learned to perform exceedingly well in nontraditional jobs, when needed during wars and emergencies, throughout our country's history.

In this book you'll meet women who are employed in such jobs. As you learn about their occupations you may want to ask some questions that will help you learn more about yourself:

- Am I able to work where I'll have constant contact with mud, dust, sparks, and grease?
- Can I stand constant noise?
- Am I allergic to any industrial substances?
- Do I mind working at heights?
- Do I want to work outdoors in all kinds of weather?
- Would I object to night-shift work?
- Am I willing to undertake physical training to qualify for a job?

By visiting a construction site, an auto repair shop, or an airplane hangar, you can see for yourself the conditions of a nontraditional workplace. If you know a man or a woman holding such a job, ask that person for job information. You can contact women's groups for additional information:

- The YWCA
- The Women's Bureau, U.S. Department of Labor
- National Organization for Women (NOW)

You can find these organizations in the white pages of the telephone directory. The Women's Bureau is listed under U.S. Government, Department of Labor.

The more you know about the world of work and about yourself, the better you can decide what will be most satisfying for your own future. We hope the experiences of the women in this book offer you some new directions, options, and choices for your own talents and abilities.

Chapter **1**

Construction

Construction is one of the largest and highest-paying industries in our country. Hourly wages are higher than in most other fields, though not yearly wages. That is so because layoffs are frequent and bad weather often interrupts construction projects. To work in this giant industry you need to be in excellent health and be willing to work outdoors, often at great heights on scaffolding. Most workers learn their trade through apprenticeship programs run jointly by unions and local contractors. You can sometimes enter one of the crafts through a combination of school courses and on-the-job training as a helper.

The three main classifications of skilled crafts are:

- Structural: operating engineers, riggers, iron workers, carpenters, stonemasons, bricklayers, concrete masons, cement masons.
- Mechanical: plumbers, pipefitters, millwrights, electricians, sheet-metal workers.
- Finishing: glaziers, painters, lathers, terrazzo workers, tile setters, paperhangers, roofers, asbestos workers, siding applicators.

Though the construction industry has been slow to accept women, their numbers have been gradually increasing. Also, harassment on the job has been, and still remains, a problem. But most women in construction agree that earning high salaries, acquiring important skills, and deriving job satisfaction make the hard work very worthwhile. For the future, construction is expected to expand, providing many new jobs.

CARPENTER

When Maryann Lane finished school, it seemed the only work choices open to her were low-paying, routine clerical jobs. In a series of these positions, she found herself limited to the typewriter and a desk, inside an office. But she realized that she wanted to work with tools and to be outdoors. Fortunately, a friend told her about a women's outreach program at a nearby YWCA. She enrolled in a program investigating high-paying jobs in nontraditional skilled trades. At the Y Center, Maryann Lane had the opportunity to learn about carpentry, and when she finished the exploratory course, she asked her counselor to arrange an appointment for her with the local carpenter's union apprenticeship officer.

The union apprenticeship officer arranged for a series of aptitude tests for Ms. Lane as well as a personal interview. Her application was evaluated by a joint committee of the union and the local contractors' organization. Ms. Lane passed all the exams and impressed the interviewing committee with her sincerity, motivation, and intelligence. The union granted her an apprenticeship and helped place her in her first job. In addition, she enrolled in special evening classes, given at union headquarters, to further her knowledge of the trade. She is now in a vocation she enjoys, earning a high salary, with excellent prospects for a promising future in a skilled craft.

If you like working outdoors and using tools and don't mind some sawdust, you may want to look more closely at carpentry. It offers high-paying, interesting work with excellent fringe benefits.

Some qualities needed by carpenters are:

- physical stamina: you'll be standing, climbing, stretching, crouching, and lifting;
- mechanical aptitude and manual dexterity: carpenters must work quickly and expertly with many hand and power tools;
- good balance: while on construction projects, you may be working on scaffolding at great heights.

To help you make your decision about entering this occupation, you could:

- take courses in carpentry at a vocational or trade school;
- enroll in wood-shop classes, as well as math, blueprint reading, and mechanical drawing, in high school;
- find a women's outreach center by calling your local YWCA; you'll find the listing in the telephone white pages.

Although the duration of outreach programs varies, they offer some or all of these services:

- explaining overall requirements of carpentry, including education, training, and job outlook;
- career counseling in both group and individual sessions;
- training with tools and materials;
- coaching for special tests and union exams;
- conditioning for physical endurance;
- helping with job or apprenticeship problems.

If you decide you are interested in becoming a carpenter, the best method for learning the trade is to get a job as an apprentice in a four-year formal apprenticeship program. Throughout the United States apprenticeship programs are administered by joint committees of the local carpenter's union and the contractors' (or employers') association. You need to submit an application for apprenticeship. You can obtain an application in several ways:

- Look in the yellow pages of the telephone book under Labor Unions or Associations. Find the carpenter's union and call, asking for the person in charge of the apprentice program. Ask that person for an application for an apprentice job.
- Consult the white pages of the telephone book for the U.S. Department of Labor, Bureau of Apprenticeship and Training. Ask at this bureau where to apply for an apprenticeship as a carpenter.
- Call the state employment service for assistance in getting an application for a carpenter's apprentice job.

When you have filed your application with the union, the joint committee representative will evaluate your record. A high school diploma is usually required. Any vocational courses you have taken and your previous work record will be weighed in deciding your eligibility for an apprenticeship. If you qualify, you'll be asked to take the next steps:

- Aptitude tests. These tests are designed to show your knowledge of vocabulary and math, your reasoning ability, and your mechanical ability.
- Oral interview. You will be interviewed by joint committee representatives, who will describe the apprenticeship program and give you a chance to ask questions. They will try to decide whether you are a good risk for the training.
- Physical exam. If you pass the above two tests, you'll be asked to take a physical exam. The committee will notify you where and when to report. You'll probably be asked to pay for this.

Congratulations! You've passed your apprenticeship entry exams. You're now ready for a job as a carpenter's apprentice. The union will help you find your first job, and you'll begin a four-year systematic program in which you'll learn the trade. In addition to learning on the job, the apprentice attends classroom training, which the joint committee sponsors and plans. Some topics covered in the classroom are care and use of tools, building code requirements, blueprint reading, and shop mathematics.

You'll be paid as an apprentice for your on-the-job training as well as your classroom instruction.

Another route for learning carpentry is through on-the-job training supplemented by evening school courses. Trainees learn skills informally by working under the supervision of experienced workers. Vocational education in the trade is offered by:

- trade and technical institutes,
- two-year community colleges,
- vocational schools.

In your new trade you'll be introduced to carpenters, the largest group of building trades workers in the industry. Carpenters are employed in every kind of construction activity, mainly in two categories, known as "rough" and "finish."

"Rough" carpenters build house frames, scaffolds, wood frames for concrete, and docks, bridges, and tunnel supports. "Finish" carpenters build stair steps, install doors and cabinets, and install wood paneling and molding. Whether "finish" or "rough," all carpenters perform their work in certain stages. Some of them are:

- reading blueprints;
- measuring work areas and materials;
- shaping wood by cutting with hand or power tools;
- joining wood structures with nails, screws, or glue;
- checking the accuracy of a job with levels, rulers, or framing squares.

The tools they use are common to all categories of carpenters. Some of the more familiar ones are:

Hand tools
- claw hammer—used to drive or pull nails;
- chisel, sharp-bladed instrument used to cut away or shape material;
- plane, bladed tool held at an angle so that it can be moved in or out to smooth or reduce the size of wood;
- saw, steel-bladed tool used to cut wood;
- ruler, made of steel;
- auger bit, used to drill wood, with a cutting edge on the bottom and a screw tip to pull it through wood.

Power tools (run by electricity, portable or stationary)
- glue gun, ejects hot glue to join small pieces of wood;
- portable screwdriver, joins wood with wood screws;
- wood-turning lathe, stationary machine that turns and shapes squares of wood into round pieces;
- plane, quick, efficient machine for smoothing and bringing down the size of wood;
- router, portable machine that makes moldings and fancy edges;
- saw, portable saw that makes cutting wood fast and easy;
- sander, portable wood-smoothing tool;
- drill, most common portable tool; used for making holes in wood.

Nails, screws, and glue are also part of the equipment carpenters employ to join or hold together the projects they build. Tools and materials are always changing, improving, and becoming safer, more efficient, and easier to use.

In spite of continuous efforts to upgrade working conditions, some disadvantages are part of this trade. Because carpentry requires the use of sharp tools in cluttered places, often on scaffolding, it can mean danger. There is always the risk of accident from falling objects, injuries inflicted by tools, and strains from heavy lifting. However, use of good safety procedures can reduce these hazards considerably. Since most carpentry is done outdoors, exposure to all kinds of weather is part of the job. In addition, the duties require long hours of standing, bending, stooping, and occasionally working in cramped quarters.

For a woman, the attitudes of men co-workers may pose special problems. Maryann Lane had to overcome some suspicion and skepticism when she started her first job. The men wondered if she had the stamina for the work and was knowledgeable enough to be productive. She overcame those negative attitudes by showing that she was competent, serious about learning, and physically capable of handling all aspects of her work.

Other women apprentices have found the hostility and harassment on the job an unpleasant burden. Also, some women are uncomfortable with the swearing or salty language they are likely to hear. Being the only woman on a construction project can be lonely and a serious drawback.

But the advantages in carpentry for women are many. Carpenters have the security of a skilled trade that can be used anywhere in the United States. The fringe benefits such as sick leave, vacations, and pensions are excellent. The average hourly rate in the 1980s for a journeyperson carpenter is $15.22, depending on locality. Starting salary for apprentices is half the journeyperson's wages. There are planned periodic raises for all workers.

Another advantage of carpentry is the future job outlook. The construction business is expected to grow, and many additional carpenters are expected to find steady employment in the next decade. Also, the trade offers ample opportunities for advancement. An experienced carpenter can move up to: supervisor, superintendent on large projects, independent contractor, estimator, trade-school instructor, or sales representative for building suppliers.

If, then, you want to consider carpentry as a career, you should be in good physical health and have some manual dexterity and mechanical aptitude. A high school diploma or equivalency diploma is required. You can learn your trade in a training program and become a skilled, highly paid worker in a rewarding job.

For additional information write to:

- United Brotherhood of Carpenters and Joiners of America
  101 Constitution Avenue, NW
  Washington, DC 20005
- Associated Builders and Contractors Inc.
  444 North Capitol Street
  Washington, DC 20001
- Associated General Contractors of America, Inc.
  1957 E Street, NW
  Washington, DC 20006

STONEMASON

The next time you admire a large, handsome stone building, you'll be enjoying the work of a stonemason. Stonemasonry is a growing, flourishing trade that goes back many centuries, and its highly skilled workers must employ accuracy, exactness, and artistry.

When Arlene Poni-Baptiste read a newspaper article about a building contractor offering jobs to apprentice stonemasons, she decided to investigate. Although her job as an arts and crafts teacher was satisfying, she wanted a career that offered her both a skill and more money. Arlene wrote a letter of application to the contractor and as a result was asked to come for an interview. During her interview she had a chance to visit the construction site, which was a cathedral. She learned that the work was outdoors and was physically strenuous. Like most construction areas, it was also dirty and noisy. However, she welcomed the chance to become an artisan in this venerable craft.

Arlene's on-the-job training is the more informal method of entering a trade; you may find this kind of job by:

ARLENE PONI-BAPTISTE, STONEMASON.

- applying directly to a stonemason or bricklaying contractor;
- applying for a job as a stonemason's helper at your state employment service;
- answering a newspaper advertisement.

Like Arlene, as an on-the-job trainee, you would work under the supervision of an experienced stonemason. This informal apprenticeship lasts four years, with periodic raises as the trainee becomes more proficient. Some of Arlene's duties are to:

- build, as well as tear down, scaffolding;
- clean tools;
- shape stones roughly;
- mix and carry mortar.

The second way of learning this trade is to apply for a formal apprenticeship of three years. Although the job duties in this program may be the same as those of the informal trainee, it requires after-work classroom study. The formal apprenticeship is usually sponsored by a joint committee of union and contractors, who work out the details of all phases of training. The program consists of 6,000 hours of work experience and 430 hours of related classroom instruction. Some classroom subjects are use of tools, mathematics, blueprint reading, and sketching.

To apply for the formal apprenticeship program, you can contact these agencies for more information:

- The state Bureau of Apprenticeship Training
- Bureau of Apprenticeship and Training, U.S. Department of Labor
- State employment service
- Women's Bureau Regional Offices, U.S. Department of Labor

Primarily, the work of a stonemason is to set stones on the exterior of buildings. In addition, she may build such structures as piers, arches, steps, and hearths.

To build these structures or set exterior stones, the mason uses two types of stone. The first is natural material such as marble, granite, limestone, and sandstone. There is also artificial stone, sometimes made of cement, marble chips, or other materials. The activities of the stonemason are varied and demand different abilities. A mason may have to cut stone to size. To do this she determines the grain of the stone and then strikes blows along a predetermined line with a mason's hammer or an abrasive saw. Like a bricklayer, the stonemason must be able to work from a set of drawings and place the stones according to specifications. On large structural projects, each properly cut stone is numbered according to the plan and drawings. Like doing a jigsaw puzzle, the stonemason fits each stone into its proper place. Derrick workers, or trainees like Arlene, assist the stonemason. She and other apprentices unload stones from trucks, placing grab hooks or lewises on them so that cranes can be used to move stones without danger of slippage. The mason sets the stone in mortar and then moves it into its final position. Checking the stone's alignment with a plumb line, the mason determines the accuracy of the setting. Finally, the mason finishes the joints between the stones with a pointing trowel to prevent water from penetrating the mortar. The stonemason must work quickly, accurately, and artistically.

Some of the tools used by masons and their apprentices are trowels, hammers, chisels, mallets, and pneumatic tools: drills, saws, and brushing tools.

Arlene finds her days strenuous, but filled with variety and challenge. She is learning her trade, and her salary is more than she could have earned teaching arts and crafts. Most of the workers on the site are men, but Arlene and the other women apprentices have not been harassed. The men on the job say, "We don't see ladies, only stone cutters." But one problem Arlene and the other women faced was finding steel-toed safety shoes in women's sizes.

For other women, however, harassment from male supervisors and co-workers in male-dominated trades can be a serious problem. The woman may be teased, ridiculed, and hazed. Occasionally, this interferes with learning, work, and even safety. Women in the trades have formed support groups to help with these experiences. For more information about these groups, look in the white pages of your telephone book for:

- National Organization for Women

- Women's Bureau, U.S. Department of Labor
- YWCA

If, then, you would like to become an apprentice stonemason you should consider these requirements. You need to be in good physical health, have a high school diploma or equivalent, and not be afraid of working at heights. Since you'll be working outdoors in both heat and cold, you should be prepared to accept those conditions. Also, you need manual dexterity and the ability to produce work quickly that is precise and meticulous.

While there is some danger from falling stones, sharp tools, and heavy lifting, good safety practices can considerable lessen these and other hazards. Safety glasses, hard hats, and steel-toed shoes are some of the equipment stonemasons wear to prevent accidents and injuries.

Some advantages of stonemasonry are the excellent hourly wage of $12.37 in the 1980s and the fringe benefits of health and life insurance, pension plans, and paid vacations. Apprentices earn half the experienced worker's wages. Salaries vary, of course, depending on the part of the country. Stonemasons can work all over the U.S., but usually they find employment in metropolitan areas where there is a need for large buildings. The indications are that the demand for stonemasons will increase in all sectors of construction, such as commercial, residential, religious, and industrial. The prospects for employment are excellent; by 1990 it is estimated that there will be a need for many additional stonemasons.

Advancement in this trade can lead to several career opportunities: supervisor; job superintendent, which usually requires additional general construction experience; estimator for stonemason contractor; or ownership of a stonemason contracting business.

If you enjoy outdoor work in a craft requiring both artistry and precision, you should investigate this centuries-old trade.

For more information about stone masonry, write to:

- International Union of Bricklayers
 and Allied Craftsmen
 815 15th Street NW
 Washington, DC 20005

- Associated General Contractors of America, Inc.
  1957 E Street, NW
  Washington, DC

GLAZIER

Sharon Holmes feels a special pride when she walks by buildings and sees her work. She's a glazier who installs and repairs windows. Her trade has given her a sense of accomplishment and fulfillment that other employment could never match. She likes working outdoors, but when she tried a sales job she found it too confining as well as too poorly paid. As a glazier she enjoys high wages, diverse work settings, and great satisfaction from completing fine handwork.

Sharon became a glazier through a time-honored method for entering a trade: with the help of a relative, her father. He was a glazier, and when he began training her brother, Sharon learned too. She had an early opportunity to become familiar with tools, and she's never been intimidated by them. As an on-the-job trainee, she worked with her father. Later she was a helper in her brother's glazing business. After several years, she felt confident enough to go out on jobs alone.

Although she prefers installing the windows in renovations of small apartment houses and replacing windows in homes, Sharon installs and repairs a wide range of glass products such as:

- mirrors,
- structural glass on building fronts,
- showcases,
- shower doors,
- tub enclosures,
- automobile windows,
- walls and ceilings,
- skylights,
- glass doors.

You can investigate this trade in several ways to determine your own interest, but you should be in good physical condition. Like other construction crafts, this trade requires standing long hours, bending, crouching, and lifting. You also need manual dexterity, patience, and accuracy. For a chance to explore and observe glaziers' work you can try:

- public high school courses in shop, math, and mechanical drawing;
- private vocational school courses in related construction trades, blueprint reading;
- women's outreach center courses in use of tools, blueprint reading;
- part-time or summer work as a helper to a glazier;
- hobby craft work, making stained glass items.

If you decide you want to pursue this career, you can do so in two ways. The first is informal on-the-job training such as Sharon Holmes undertook when she worked with her father. In this way you would work under the supervision of an experienced glazier, progressing from simple to more complicated tasks until you learned the trade. Generally, it takes three to four years to complete the training. To find an on-the-job training situation you can:

- apply directly to a glazier, either a contractor or in a factory. Check for these companies in the yellow pages under Glass or Glaziers;
- inquire for such a job at the state employment service;
- look for help-wanted ads in the newspapers for helper to a glazier.

The other route is to enter a formal apprenticeship program. This consists of three years of carefully planned activity combining 6,000 hours of shop training with 144 hours each year of classroom instruction. For information on applying for this type of apprenticeship, contact:

- The state office of the Bureau of Apprenticeship and Training, U.S. Department of Labor
- The state employment office
- International Brotherhood of Painters and Allied Trades. Look in the yellow pages under Labor Unions or Associations for the local telephone number and address.

After applying, you'll be evaluated by a joint labor-management committee, which will check your education, previous work experience, and health. If you're accepted you begin as an apprentice, starting at half the salary of the journeyperson glazier. You receive periodic raises as you progress and become more skilled. Your classroom courses include:

- selection of glass for different purposes,
- theory of glass manufacturing,
- erection of scaffolding,
- blueprinting,
- tools and their maintenance.

As a glazier your job would be to install, fit, and cut glass either at a construction site or in factory. In doing so, you would:

- cut glass to fit, breaking off excess pieces by hand or with a special tool;
- put a bit of putty into the wood or metal frame;
- press the glass into place in the frame;
- fasten the glass where necessary with wire clippers or triangular metal points;
- apply another strip of putty on the outside edges to seal the glass into place and make it moistureproof.

Large pieces of glass are sometimes set in mastic or other flexible and weatherproof material. It is the glazier's job to know what kind of material is needed for each situation and how to use it.

In addition to knowing setting materials, the glazier may have to cut metal drains and metal face moldings for installation of storefronts. Also, she may have to install or repair a wide variety of windows such as opening sash, sliding sash, pivoted sash, double sash, or casement windows. Great care is needed when the glazier works on these windows so that there's a "floating fit" of $1/16$ inch for small installations to $1/4$ inch for larger windows. Unless she does her work with patience and care, the glass will be subject to strain and may crack and shatter.

Glaziers also work in factories, where they process glass by: cutting, grinding, and polishing. The products they complete by installing glass may be prefabricated windows, prefabricated doors, or mirrors.

In factory settings conditions differ from the construction site in that the work is indoors. Some of these facilities may be pleasant, well lighted and ventilated, but others may not be so.

Whether in a factory or on a construction site, all glaziers use similar tools. Some of them are:

- Hand tools: glass cutters, putty knives, hammers, metal cutters, screwdrivers.
- Power tools for cutting, grinding, and polishing.

In addition to tools, special equipment is needed for unusual situations. On jobs requiring plate glass in stores and in high-rise buildings, special power equipment is used to handle the glass and move it into place.

The advantages and rewards of the glazier's craft are several. First, the average hourly wage in the mid-1980s was $12.00 and was expected to rise. Different parts of the country, however, have varying rates. Most glaziers work a 40-hour week with overtime beyond those hours. Even though it is a relatively small field, an increase in employment is expected. The trend toward using more glass in construction of commercial and residential building means an increased demand for glaziers, not only for installation but repair work as well. Work is available anywhere in the country, but demand is greatest in metropolitan areas.

There are, of course, drawbacks in this trade. There's danger of cuts from glass and sharp tools. Sharon Holmes and other glaziers wear gloves, safety glasses, and hard hats to protect them from flying glass. Like other construction workers, you may have to operate on scaffolding at great heights where there's danger from falling tools and other materials. Good safety practices lessen the risks and dangers.

Unfortunately, another unpleasant feature of the trade can be hostile reactions from men unused to working with women in a predominantly male trade. Sharon Holmes has found that initial resistance is overcome as women prove themselves competent workers. But often women may find themselves shut out of the men's camaraderie as well as becoming the objects of hazing and hostility. Ms. Holmes believes strongly that women should reach out for support and join with other women in the trades. To find such groups in your area you can:

- ask the local YWCA if they have a women's outreach group;
- check the local National Organization for Women chapter;
- inquire at the state employment service for information about a local women's trade organization.

At the end of your apprenticeship you become a full-fledged journeyperson by whatever route you have followed. Once you are a journeyperson you can look forward to several promotion opportunities: job supervisor for a glazier, job superintendent for a large glazing contractor, job estimator for a glazier, or independent glazier.

For women who have the patience for completing a task with care and accuracy, becoming a glazier means having a trade that brings feelings of accomplishment, provides well-paying work, and can be performed throughout the country.

For more information you can write to:

- International Brotherhood of Painters and Allied Trades
  1750 New York Avenue, NW
  Washington, DC 20006

PAINTER

For Oceania Bliss, being a free-lance construction painter has meant the freedom to move around the country and, while doing so, earn a good living. She's had the choice, when a project ends, of staying in an area and looking for another job or of moving to a different city and state. For the past ten years she's been a journeyperson painter, and although she realizes that not every woman wants to be as mobile as she is, she recommends painting as a career. Although it's hard work, she says it pays well, offers plenty of variety with each new job, and can lead to owning your own business.

During summer school vacations, Oceania Bliss worked as a painter's helper and had a chance to familiarize herself with the craft. After finishing her education she tried the restaurant business and the advertising field. But she decided that being a

CONSTRUCTION   21

OCEANIA BLISS, CONSTRUCTION PAINTER.

painter offered her the money and the flexibility she preferred. She served an informal apprenticeship as an on-the-job trainee with a painting contractor. For three years, under the guidance of experienced painters, she learned her trade until she became skilled enough to go out on her own as a free-lance painter. She usually joins a crew as part of a painting contractor's work team when they are completing a building project.

If you'd like to explore this trade, you should be in good shape physically, because you'll be standing most of the day, as well as climbing, bending, crouching, and lifting heavy equipment. In addition, you have to work for hours with your arms raised over your head. Some other requirements you need are manual dexterity; nonallergy to paint, varnish, and turpentine; and good color sense.

There are several ways you can get hands-on experience in this field:

- take courses in industrial arts in high school;
- enroll in a private vocational or trade school for courses in painting and related subjects;
- practice painting in your own home;
- find part-time or summer work as a helper for a painting contractor.

If you decide this is the trade you want to learn, there are two ways you can become a full-fledged painter, or journeyperson. Like Oceania Bliss, you can start as a helper or on-the-job trainee for a painting contractor. This means that for about three years you would work under the guidance of experienced painters and gradually learn all the skills you need. Some of the duties of a helper or trainee are to:

- carry equipment and paint from trucks to the job site,
- set up ladders, scaffolds, and other gear,
- remove old paint from the surface to be painted,
- mask areas not to be painted,
- cover the workplace with drop cloths,
- keep painters supplied with paint,
- clean brushes and other equipment,
- drive the truck.

Many journeyperson painters began as helpers and on-the-job trainees. More than in any other construction trade, painters are accepted without a formal apprenticeship. However, a formal apprenticeship is highly recommended as the best way to succeed in this occupation. To apply for formal apprenticeship, contact:

- The state apprenticeship agency or bureau
- The state employment service for help in finding the proper agency or local union to contact
- National Joint Painting, Decorating and Drywall Finishing Apprenticeship and Training Committee, 1709 New York Avenue, NW, Suite 110, Washington, DC 20006

To secure an apprenticeship, you'll be evaluated by a joint labor-management committee. They'll be looking for:

- education: high school diploma or equivalent; industrial arts or vocational school courses in math, chemistry, or any construction trades subject;
- experience: part-time and summer work should be included;
- health: good physical condition is a must.

If you are approved, you enter a formal program combining carefully planned work experience for three years with related classroom instruction. Some of the classroom courses are:

- chemistry,
- color coordination,
- cost estimating,
- color mixing,
- paperhanging,
- related trades: carpentry and plastering (since the painter follows the carpenter and plasterer, she may have to cover up or correct their mistakes).

A journeyperson painter takes several steps even before painting is begun. She prepares the surface for the paint and mixes the correct amounts of materials in the required color. Some of the tools she uses are electric sander, blowtorch, putty knife, wood scraper, caulking gun, hammer, pliers, chisel, screwdriver, and paint mixers.

In preparing a surface, she removes old paint and grease. If the surface has holes, she fills them, as well as any cracks or joints. To do this, she uses putty, plaster, or some other sealer to smooth out the surface. Very often she applies a prime coat or a sealer to the surface to make the final paint coat look smooth and well blended.

Once the surface is prepared, the painter chooses premixed paint or prepares paint by mixing amounts of pigment (color), oil, and thinning and drying substances. The final step is applying the paint with a brush, a spray gun, or a roller.

A skilled painter must know her equipment and when to use each type. She knows that brushes should have bristles of the proper shape and size for the job. The brushes should be soft and have tapered edges, with good balance and comfortable handles. Rollers are either dip or fountain pressure types. The spray gun is generally used for large surfaces where lacquer or high-gloss enamel is to be used.

A related trade, paperhanging, is often studied by apprentices, and many painters do this work. As in painting, the paperhanger prepares the surface. She may have to seal a new surface with sizing. If old paper is removed, any holes or cracks beneath it must be filled with plaster. After the surface is carefully made ready, the paperhanger measures, cuts, and pastes the wallpaper. Last, the pasted wallpaper is placed on the wall, carefully positioned, and smoothed down to remove air bubbles.

Owning her own tools and brushes represents an expense for painters, but for Oceania Bliss it has meant the freedom to operate independently in different places and situations. Since she has a wide range of equipment, she has diversified and enlarged her job options. She has done construction painting and also worked on interiors and exteriors of houses and on outdoor signs and murals. She says the only disadvantage in her work is the "shuffle to get jobs" in unfamiliar places.

In the past ten years, Oceania has noticed that women have been accepted much more matter of factly by all-male crews. In her experience, crews have been working more smoothly with women, and as her co-workers realize her expertise, harassment has disappeared for her. For other women workers this has not been so. Women in trades where men predominate may be teased, ridiculed, and obstructed in learning and working. For help in handling such situations, contact:

- The local YWCA women's outreach program
- The local chapter of the National Organization for Women

Completing your apprenticeship will offer you several important advantages. First, the wages: in the 1980s the average hourly wage for painters and paperhangers is $14.00. Apprentices earn half the journeyperson's salary. These wages vary in different sections of the country. Second, painters work a regular 40-hour week with extra pay for overtime. In addition, employment of painters and paperhangers is expected to grow as fast as the average for all occupations in the 1980s. Increased construction in the business and industrial segments means a need for more painters on these commercial projects. This trend counters the tendency for inexperienced homeowners to do their own work.

You should also be aware of some of the disadvantages in this trade:

- danger of falling from ladders or scaffolds—good safety practices can reduce this hazard;
- loss of work because of bad weather;
- inhaling toxic fumes from paint, varnish, and other materials; wearing a mask may be necessary.

A journeyperson in this trade can look forward to advancement to positions such as supervisor for a contracting firm, estimator for a painting and decorating contractor, superintendent on a large contract painting job, or independent painting contractor.

As part of the construction crafts, painting offers employment throughout the country at good wages, with opportunities for advancement.

For more information, contact:

- Painting and Decorating Contractors of America
  7223 Lee Highway
  Falls Church, VA 22046

Chapter II

Electric Power

Our highly industrialized society depends on utility companies to keep us supplied with essential electric power. In spite of the continuing need, however, employment in this industry is expected to increase only slowly. But if you have a nontraditional job in one of the three electric power divisions of a utility plant, your job will be secure. You'll be needed even when the economy is weak, and electric power companies seldom lay off workers.

Some nontraditional jobs in the three divisions are:

- Power plant: switchboard operators, boiler operators, auxiliary equipment operators, control room operators, watch engineers
- Transmission and distribution: cable splicers, line installers, load dispatchers, substation operators, ground helpers
- Customer service: meter readers, meter repairers and installers

In this field, you can get training on the job, though employers usually want applicants with a high school diploma. Utility plants operate 24 hours a day, and workers have to be available for emergency duty. Most plants are covered by unions, and salaries in the utility industry are higher than similar jobs in private industry.

CABLE SPLICER

"A lot more realistic," is how Betty Davis describes her salary as an on-the-job trainee cable splicer in the electric transmission and

BETTY DAVIS, CABLE SPLICER

distribution division of a large utility company. And a more realistic salary was just what Ms. Davis needed, because her previous jobs as a sales clerk, a cashier, and a nursery school aide certainly had failed to yield a livelihood. When she saw a newspaper advertisement for a cable splicer trainee job with an electric company, at a good salary, she applied to the personnel office. A high school diploma was required, but no other special education or experience was needed. In the past only men were considered for splicers, but affirmative action laws, both state and federal, have opened this occupation for women.

Betty Davis learned that the work was done outdoors in all kinds of weather and required heavy lifting, bending, and crouching. Splicers also made repairs in cramped underground tunnels below the streets where the cables were laid. The interviewer tested her for physical stamina as well as mechanical aptitude and manual dexterity.

Neither the heavy lifting, nor prospects of working in cold

weather, nor functioning underground in cramped spaces faze Ms. Davis. She enjoys being outdoors, and with proper clothing bad weather doesn't bother her. Also, working with her hands and with tools gives her a special satisfaction even in the cramped underground tunnels.

If you'd like to find out whether you'd like this work, you can do so in several ways:

- Find a part-time or summer job as a helper or laborer in a power plant.
- Take a course in repairing electrical devices in a women's outreach center such as those sponsored by the YWCA.
- Take courses in blueprint reading and mechanical drawing in a trade or vocational school.
- Choose electric shop courses in high school.

If after investigating the trade you decide to become a cable splicer, you can look for a trainee's or helper's job by:

- applying directly to the personnel office of the local electric utility company;
- checking newspaper advertisements;
- inquiring at the state employment service.

If you are hired you will, like most cable splicers, receive on-the-job training by working under the supervision of an experienced splicer. Helpers or trainees may:

- open manholes;
- place the splicer's platform in position;
- supply the splicer with tools and equipment;
- tend a small gasoline engine that pumps water from underground tunnels;
- cut lead tubing with a hacksaw;
- drive a panel truck.

When breaking concrete to reach underground cable conduits, Betty Davis has had to use pick and shovel as well as power tools. Under close supervision, she's learning to use the pneumatic jackhammer. Of course, she and her fellow splicers use safety equipment including hard hats, safety glasses, steel-toed shoes, and gloves. It takes about four years to learn the job thoroughly and become a full-fledged or journeyperson cable splicer.

The journeyperson cable splicer may work on poles or in underground tunnels. But whatever the work site, she must first read and interpret her service orders and circuit diagrams to determine the proper splicing specifications. Then the splicer connects individual wires within the cable or rearranges wires when lines have to be changed. Some of the splicer's tasks are to:

- make splices by twisting, soldering, or joining wires and cables with small hand tools, epoxy, and mechanical equipment;
- place insulation at each splice over the conductor;
- seal the splice with a lead sleeve or cover it with some other protective covering.

Furthermore, cable splicers spend much of their time routinely checking for maintenance and repair of power lines. They continuously inspect to make sure that the insulation on cables is in good condition. Both splicers and their helpers use tools such as knives, hammers, pliers, hacksaws, wrenches, screwdrivers, and chisels.

When a wire or cable breaks, or an underground duct collapses, the splicers must make emergency repairs as quickly as possible. These situations are common in parts of the country that have hurricanes, tornadoes, earthquakes, and heavy snowfalls.

Working under pressure as well as in more routine conditions can be hazardous. There is danger from electric shocks as well as falls. These, however, have been greatly reduced by safety precautions developed over the years. Some special safety features are insulated tools, special gloves, safety belts, and body belts. Accidents are kept to a minimum when splicers observe established safety regulations.

Splicers in the electric power industry enjoy some excellent advantages. They include:

- Salaries: average per hour in the 1980s ranged from $8.40 to $12.10, with trainees starting at half the journeyperson's wage.

- Hours: a regular 40-hour week, but some utility employees must work shifts. Splicers are on call for emergencies.
- Paid holidays.
- Sick leave.
- Insurance: medical and life.
- Retirement programs.

A special bonus for those in the electric power industry is that layoffs are rare. When a splicer is in excess, she's usually given a choice of transferring to another area or being placed in a different job in the same location. Power companies seldom discharge workers. This policy, however, may limit the number of openings available to outsiders.

The demand for cable splicers is expected to grow about as fast as the average for all occupations in the United States through the mid-1990s. Most of the openings that do occur will be to replace workers who retire, leave, or transfer.

Betty Davis has found her more experienced men co-workers cooperative and helpful. Her supervisor is so pleased with her work that he wishes he had "more workers just like her." Because she's had such a positive experience, Ms. Davis has no hesitation in recommending a cable splicing job for other women.

"You can always clean up after work and be your own pretty self," she says about the grime and dirt you find in the workplace.

Women in the male-dominated jobs often have to prove themselves capable and efficient before they gain acceptance by their co-workers. Men can be suspicious, hostile, and skeptical. If you decide to enter this trade you should be aware that these attitudes can cause problems for you. But Betty Davis has some words of encouragement: "Do what makes you happy and don't let other people discourage you."

For support and help in dealing with harassment, contact:

- The YWCA women's outreach group
- National Organization for Women

When you've finished your training and become a journeyperson cable splicer you can look forward to advancement as a supervisor or instructor of new employees.

To be a cable splicer in an industry that offers stable employment, benefits, and a varied workday, you should have good physical health, manual dexterity, and mechanical aptitude. You have to enjoy working outdoors in all kinds of weather. You also need to be able to work in the cramped underground vaults. For more information, contact the unions to which most cable splicers belong:

- Utility Workers Union of America AFL-CIO
  815 16th Street, NW
  Washington, DC 20006
- International Brotherhood of Electrical Workers
  1125 15th Street, NW
  Washington, DC 20005

Chapter III

Telephone

The vast telephone industry makes communication possible in every hamlet in the United States. Employment in this industry is safe and stable and offers good wages, excellent benefits, and career advancement. In addition, telephone companies are recruiting women to fill skilled craft jobs. Despite trends to replace workers with labor-saving devices, there will be a growing need for skilled personnel because of expansion of the industry.

CENTRAL OFFICE TECHNICIAN

"Typing is working! If you don't type, you don't work! Or so I thought," says Eileen Piesco, a central office technician for her local telephone company. Just a few years ago she was confined to a desk and typewriter all day for the same company. Though it was dull, routine, and low-paying, she never doubted that typing was proper "woman's work."

But then her company offered women technical or craft jobs, previously held only by men, and she decided to investigate. She found these craft jobs paid better and were more varied and interesting, and she decided to take the opportunity to change from the clerical to a technical field. She also liked the surroundings of the central office technicians. They worked in clean, well-lighted, air-conditioned rooms in central office buildings. Ms. Piesco's company had the same transfer policy as other telephone companies: they offered her all the necessary training for her new job, both classroom and on-the-job.

Before making the change, however, she was screened by the

personnel department. Since technicians need certain abilities, she had to be tested to determine her potential.

Although no heavy lifting is necessary in this job, a technician must be able to meet certain physical demands. Some of them are standing all day, climbing ladders occasionally, reaching or stooping once in a while, and lifting light equipment.

In addition, one of the most important physical requirements is good color vision. Since most telephone wires are color coded, the technician must be able to distinguish colors accurately.

Eileen took tests to measure her manual dexterity and mechanical aptitude. The technician must use small tools with precision and accuracy while working with fine wires. Eileen Piesco passed all these tests and was accepted for training. She began her new career in the entry-level job called frame wirer or frame attendant.

If you would like to find out whether this kind of work would suit you, you can:

- apply for a summer or part-time job in a business that repairs or sells electric or electronic equipment;
- investigate courses in the use of hand tools at a women's outreach center such as those offered by the YWCA;
- take classes in the principles of electricity and electrical repair at a vocational or trade school;
- enroll in electric shop, mechanical drawing, or physics classes in high school.

If you find that you enjoy working with hand tools and would like to try the job as central office technician, you should apply directly to the personnel office of your telephone company. You can telephone and ask for an application and appointment to be considered for the job.

Most telephone companies require a high school diploma for the technician's job. Related courses in repair and maintenance of electrical equipment may add to your qualifications, giving you an advantage over other applicants. If your background and screening tests show that you have potential for a central office technician's work, you'll be hired when an opening becomes available.

When you do start the job, you are trained for your tasks as a frame wirer. You learn on the job, working with experienced employees, and receive classroom instruction. Your job is working on wires running from outside telephone lines and cables to the central office. The wires have to be connected to central office frames. The frames have terminal lugs mounted on them, and each lug has a specific number. The frames contain one pair of wires for each telephone connected to that central office. The duties of the frame wirer include:

- connecting new telephones by soldering the customer's wires to the terminal lugs on the frame;
- disconnecting a telephone by removing the wires from the terminal;
- changing a customer's telephone number by reconnecting the wires to a different set of terminal lugs;
- inspecting and repairing frames for breaks or loose wires;
- helping other craft workers locate and correct malfunctions.

Among the tools the frame wirer uses are pliers, screwdrivers, and soldering irons.

New frame wirers train from six months to one year. After one or two years of satisfactory performance, the frame wirer may be selected for further training as a central office technician.

The main duties of a central office technician are to examine, test, and repair equipment that automatically connects lines when customers dial numbers. To do so, she may have to:

- set up or install complicated switching equipment following plant diagrams or blueprints;
- make connections for incoming or outgoing lines;
- test the system;
- maintain and repair central office switching and automatic message accounting equipment;
- find and analyze service disruptions;
- clear up trouble inside or outside the central office by directing repair technicians.

Some of the tools used by the central office technician are: pliers, screwdrivers, soldering irons, capacity meters, and wall meters.

In addition to manual dexterity and mechanical aptitude, a central office technician needs the ability and self-discipline to follow detailed written instructions and to complete a task without close supervision. In fact, Eileen Piesco enjoys this aspect of the position because making decisions and managing her time adds interest and prestige to her job.

Another important aspect of the work of a central office technician or frame wirer is the capacity to function as part of a team. She has to be able to cooperate with other technical employees to solve complex problems disrupting service. Close cooperation among technical personnel is important in maintaining equipment at peak performance.

For their skills and abilities, central office technicians enjoy several advantages. Some of them are:

- Salaries: In the 1980s the average hourly pay was $12.50 per hour.
- Hours: The workweek is 8 hours per day, 5 days per week. There is extra pay for overtime, work on Sundays or holidays, and night work.
- Vacations: Employees receive paid vacations depending on length of service.
- Fringe benefits: Workers are entitled to paid sick leave, medical and dental insurance, retirement disability pensions, and participation in an employee stock ownership plan.

The workplace of central office technicians is not only clean, well lit, and air-conditioned, but also very safe. Central office technicians are strictly trained to follow safety practices. Consequently, they have one of the best safety records for workers in all U.S. companies.

Another boon for employees in the telephone industry is the well-established custom of retaining employees if they are in excess in a particular location. Telephone companies retrain their workers or transfer them to other jobs or localities to avoid layoffs.

Some disadvantages of being a central office technician are:

- Shift work: You may be required to work night shifts, weekends, or holidays.

- Emergencies: Employees are subject to twenty-four-hour call.
- Noise: Some equipment continually produces sounds that workers must learn to block out.

A drawback of holding a job previously done only by men is the resentment of some male co-workers toward the newcomers. Eileen Piesco found that the women who were first in these positions encountered most of the hostility. After a short time she found that most of her men co-workers became accustomed to women on the job. Cooperation, she says, has improved as more women routinely hold these jobs.

Openings for the central office technician job are expected to increase slowly through the 1980s. However, there will be many thousands of new openings each year as experienced workers transfer, retire, or leave for other reasons. There are also conflicting future trends for this job category.

Advances in technology will stimulate and increase the demand for installation of more equipment in the central offices; but conversion to automatic equipment means that fewer maintenance and repair personnel will be needed.

Promotion and advancement in a telephone company are based on satisfactory performance. With promotion, the company offers training for the new job with combination on-the-job and classroom instruction. A central office technician can advance to central office supervisor, wire chief, job supervisor of city exchange, administrative staff worker, or engineering assistant.

Should you decide to work as a central office technician, you'll be able to find job opportunities throughout the country. You need to have manual dexterity, mechanical aptitude, and good color vision and to be able to work as part of a team. The rewards are a well-paying job with excellent fringe benefits and opportunities for advancement.

For more information, contact the unions to which most telephone workers belong:

- Communications Workers of America
  1925 K Street, NW
  Washington, DC 20006

- International Brotherhood of Electrical Workers
  1125 15th Street, NW
  Washington, DC 20005
- Telecommunications International Union
  2341 Whitney Avenue
  Hamden, CT 06518

LINE INSTALLER

Sometimes she's thirty feet above the ground swaying gently in a sky bucket, sometimes she's hanging by a belt high up on a telephone pole, but no matter where she is, Kathy Wood is working on a rugged job she loves. She's a telephone line installer, and with her partner the cable splicer she constructs and maintains telephone wires and cables running between individual telephones and central offices.

As a former service representative for a telephone company, she had no idea of changing her work until her company offered craft and technician's jobs to women. What she learned about these positions, previously held only by men, persuaded her to ask for a transfer. First, she found that line installers earn much more money than service representatives. Second, in contrast to her routine desk job, line installers work outdoors, moving from place to place and doing a variety of tasks. She also liked the fact that line installers have plenty of opportunity to use their own judgment and work with a minimum of supervision. And finally, the telephone company would pay for the training to make the change.

Before being accepted for the training program, Kathy was screened by the personnel department. Candidates for this occupation need certain qualifications to meet the demands of the job:

- Physical condition: The job requires considerable climbing, reaching, pulling, lifting, and walking. A line installer should possess stamina, agility, and excellent health.
- Personality: To work with little supervision, a line installer should be dependable, stable, and alert and be able to function as part of a team.

KATHY WOOD, TELEPHONE LINE INSTALLER.

- Vision: Since the installer works with color-coded wires, she needs good color perception as well as normal vision.
- Manual dexterity and mechanical aptitude: Needed to work skillfully, quickly, and accurately with fine wires, hand tools, and other equipment.

No matter what the weather—rain, sleet, or snow—the line installer may have to be on the job. There's no way of knowing when storms, hurricanes, or earthquakes will knock down telephone poles and disrupt lines. Kathy Wood, as a line installer, must be on call to work during emergencies to restore telephone service.

If you want to test your own interest and motivation for this job, you can try several approaches:

- Apply for a part-time or summer job as a helper or laborer with a telephone company or a private contractor doing line installation. These companies are listed in the yellow pages under Contractors, Telephone Line.
- Take high school courses in electricity, machine shop, math, and physics.
- Enroll in a vocational or trade school for classes in blueprint reading, mechanical drawing, and repair of electrical devices.
- Investigate resources in a women's outreach center (often in the YWCA) for training in the use of hand tools and basic principles of electricity.
- Pursue hobbies requiring a knowledge of electricity and electronics, such as ham radio operator.

In the event that you decide you want the job of line installer, you can apply directly to the personnel office of your telephone company. Also, you can:

- contact private companies installing telephone lines;
- consult the state employment service;
- check newspaper help wanted ads for jobs as helper or trainee line installer.

In the personnel office, the interviewer will evaluate your employment history and education. Most telephone companies prefer to hire inexperienced applicants with a high school education. If there are openings, you will be given tests to assess your capabilities. If you are hired, you will be paid while the company trains you.

Combining classroom and on-the-job instruction, you will have the opportunity to learn your craft. Some classroom subjects are:

- company policies and procedures,
- safety regulations,
- electrical and electronic theory,
- blueprint reading,
- power equipment operation,
- line practice.

Classrooms often duplicate actual working conditions, even to telephone poles. You'll be taught to climb the poles and work safely before you go out with a line crew to gain experience under close supervision of skilled workers. As a trainee you may:

- assist in raising and removing poles,
- load and unload tools and materials from trucks,
- unreel flexible stranded wire,
- run cables between communication points.

It usually takes four to five years to learn the job of line installer and reach the top salary step. However, even when thoroughly experienced, a line installer never stops learning new operations and techniques. Advanced, developing technology means learning new methods of working and using updated equipment.

After a line installer gains enough skill and experience, she works in the field with the cable splicer and other crew members. She will:

- construct new telephone lines by erecting poles and towers or laying line in underground conduits. The line installer uses power tools to dig holes or trenches. Then she helps erect poles or towers to support cables and wires.
- string wires and cables on poles or underground. She may use sky buckets or other power aerial lifts, or climb poles to place cables in order to complete circuits between individual telephone lines and the central office.

- join sections of powerline, splicing, soldering, and insulating conductors and related wiring.
- repair and maintain existing lines. This is the major work of the installer. She checks for wire or cable breaks, downed poles, and slack or worn lines. She may clean and resplice damaged wires and reseal connections.

After the line installer has placed the wires and cables, her partner the cable splicer connects them to complete the circuits that connect the telephone and the central office. Like the line installer, the splicer also works on aerial platforms and poles, in manholes, basements, and trenches. Her main duties are to connect wires within the cables and rearrange wires when lines have to be changed. She also installs terminal enclosures or boxes for access to cables for connection purposes.

The tools line installers use include:

- Hand tools: pliers, wrenches, screwdrivers, soldering irons, torches.
- Power tools: tree trimmers, hole diggers, and plows that dig trenches, lay and then cover cable.

Although being a line installer is strenuous and demanding work, if the job suits you it offers excellent advantages:

- Earnings: Average hourly rate in the mid-1980s was $10.28 per hour, varying in different sections of the country.
- Hours: A 40-hour workweek with extra pay for overtime and Sundays. During emergencies, line installers are on call. Also telephone employees may have to work different shifts.
- Vacations: Annual, varying with length of service.
- Paid holidays: From eight to eleven days, depending on the company.
- Paid sick leave.
- Group health and life insurance.
- Pension plans.
- Job security: Telephone companies seldom lay off workers. They prefer to retrain or transfer excess workers.

You should also be aware of the disadvantages:

- working in extreme weather conditions;
- repairing equipment in emergencies may require long, exhausting hours;
- risk of falls, electric shocks, and cuts from sharp tools; accidents are kept to a minimum by strict observance of safety procedures as well as use of hard hats, gloves, safety glasses, and insulated tools.

There may be other disadvantages for women who work in nontraditional jobs. Men who aren't accustomed to women as coworkers can create an atmosphere of hostility and tension. Kathy Wood cautions women to expect practical jokes, teasing, and suspicion as some men adjust their attitudes. She has observed, though, that very few men stay prejudiced for long after working with competent, confident women. She also cautions that you'll hear plenty of salty language and "you can't be prudish." She says that women in nontraditional jobs need a good sense of humor and patience.

For support and help in dealing with difficult problems of harassment, check with:

- National Organization for Women.
- YWCA women's outreach groups.
- Women's trade organizations: the state employment service may help you find a local group.

After satisfactory performance as a line installer, you could advance to several positions, such as line crew supervisor, telephone installer, or central office equipment installer.

Employment opportunities for line installers are expected to increase at a moderately slow rate, despite the fact that telephone companies will extend lines and cables into suburban areas. This is so because redesigned equipment and new technology enable companies to provide efficient service using fewer personnel. Nevertheless, job openings will occur to replace workers who leave, retire, or move into other occupations. The best opportunities for line installers are developing in small towns rather than big cities, because of the many miles of cable that have to be installed and maintained in rural areas.

For women in good physical condition who like working

outdoors and have mechanical aptitude and manual dexterity, being a line installer is rewarding work with excellent benefits and job security. For more information, write to:

- Communications Workers of America
  1925 K Street, NW
  Washington, DC 20006
- International Brotherhood of Electrical Workers
  1125 15th Street, NW
  Washington, DC 20005
- Telecommunications International Union
  2341 Whitney Avenue
  Hamden, CT 06518

TELEPHONE INSTALLER

"You don't have to an electronic genius to handle a screwdriver. I never handled tools before this job, and now that I do I think it's fun." That's how Mary Ellen Mathews, a telephone installer, enthusiastically explains her job.

Originally a telephone business representative, she worked in very different circumstances than she does now. Mainly, she was on the phone dealing with business problems of customers. In an office, at her desk, she worked with other business representatives. Now her duties take her out to homes, basements, yards, and even high on telephone poles. She's meeting different people, doing skilled technical work, and filling her busy days with variety and challenge.

Each morning, Mary Ellen meets with her foreman and gets her assignments. Then she drives off in her well-equipped panel truck and is on her own for the rest of the day. Every installation raises new problems because of unusual, diverse locations and people. In the field she uses the same tact and diplomacy she employed as a business representative. In addition, her experience and training have prepared her to solve difficulties without supervision.

Like many other women, Ms. Mathews took the opportunity to change to a craft and technical occupation as a result of an upgrading and transfer program. Telephone companies have changed their policies and are now recruiting women for careers once open only to men. The main benefit to Ms. Mathews is that

MARY ELLEN MATHEWS, TELEPHONE INSTALLER

she earns 25 percent more than she did in former job. She can also look forward to advancement and training that will lead to more responsible, complex, and still higher-paying jobs. Does a position requiring mechanical ability as well dealing with the public appeal to you? If you want to look more closely at the possibilities, you can:

- take math, physics, and shopwork in high school;
- explore courses in a women's outreach center in the use of hand tools, principles of electricity, or repair of electrical devices; you can find these centers by inquiring at your local YWCA or the state employment service;
- study mechanical drawing and blueprint reading at a vocational or trade school;
- build or assemble electronic kits as a hobby.

Installing telephones requires different qualifications than those for office or sales jobs. Among them are:

- Physical: good vision and color perception to manipulate fine color-coded wires; stamina to bend, crouch, kneel, climb, and lift up to 60 pounds.
- Personality: ability to work independently and reliably as well as treat the public courteously and patiently.
- Manual dexterity and mechanical aptitude: good eye-hand coordination to work with small hand drills, screwdrivers, soldering irons, and staple guns.

If you've decided you'd like to apply for an installer's job, contact the personnel or employment office of a telephone company. Since these companies prefer to hire inexperienced people and train them, your education and aptitude tests will be considered. In addition, the interviewer will be looking for a neat-looking person with a pleasant personality because in this job you deal with the public. Your high school or vocational school diploma will add to your qualifications. You'll also be given tests to judge your physical and mechanical abilities. If you qualify, but the company has no immediate openings for installers, you may be assigned to another position until an opening does occur. It is common practice to transfer workers to installation or repair from other job classifications. Trainees often come from the ranks of operators, clerical workers, line installers, and cable splicers.

When you do become a trainee installer, you will study first in a classroom where actual job conditions are duplicated. The courses include blueprint and circuit diagram reading, electrical and electronic theory, installation procedures, and pole climbing.

During your apprenticeship you'll get practice in connecting wires and other related tasks. After mastering the basics, you'll be assigned as a helper to experienced workers on actual job sites.

If you live in a rural area where the telephone company doesn't have its own training facilities, the company will send you to a technical or vocational school, paying your tuition and travel expenses.

On the job site, senior crew members will help you learn your craft thoroughly and with strict safety procedures. Training usually takes several months before you're able to go out alone and install telephones competently and safely.

Although Mary Ellen Mathews installs residential telephones in a large city, installers in less populated areas work both in businesses and homes. Their duties are to:

- install, rearrange, or remove telephones;
- assemble equipment and install wiring on the premises of customers;
- connect telephones to outside service wires, climbing poles if necessary; or to wire closets or terminals that may be located in basements;
- test equipment;
- keep accurate and detailed records of all work undertaken;
- demonstrate to customers various kinds of telephone equipment and services.

An installer specializing in more complicated systems receives additional training and is called a PBX installer. She does most of the work in large buildings such as offices, hotels, hospitals, and factories.

Her duties include:

- using hand tools and equipment such as signal generators, ohmmeters, and oscilloscopes;

- connecting wires from terminals to switchboards and power cabinets;
- testing for proper operation of installations;
- setting up equipment for wire and microwave transmission of mobile radiotelephones and other complicated devices;
- suggesting additional or alternative service as well as explaining rates and charges to customers.

To qualify for more skilled jobs as well as keep up with new technology, craft workers take training throughout their careers. Although companies offer instruction, the latest developments are also taught by colleges and universities and by state telephone associations.

An installer in the telephone industry can look forward to excellent job benefits:

- Earnings: the average hourly rate for telephone and PBX installers in the 1980s was $13.02.
- Hours: a 40-hour, 5-day week, with extra pay for holidays, night work, and Sundays.
- Paid vacations according to length of service.
- Paid sick leave.
- Paid holidays.
- Fringe benefits: life, medical, and dental insurance; retirement and disability pensions; stock ownership plans.

On the other hand, being a telephone installer can have disadvantages:

- Conditions: You may have to work outdoors in severe weather. While indoors, you may be in damp, unlighted, and unventilated places.
- Hazards: Danger from falls or electric shocks. Good safety practices reduce these risks.
- Emergency duty: Telephone company employees are on call in emergencies.

For the future, chances are good for steady work for telephone and PBX installers through the 1990s. Employment is expected to increase about as fast as the average for all occupations. Most future openings will be the result of growth, but retirements, resignations, and transfers will also provide many new jobs. The volume of telephone business is expected to rise because of expanding popularity of extension phones, increasing use of specialized telephone equipment, and development of more sophisticated devices.

For the installer interested in promotion, there are a number of possibilities based on level of skill, technical knowledge, and length of service. If an installer meets standards for promotion, she must also be willing to continue her career education indefinitely. Science and engineering are constantly making advances in the telephone industry that mean new ways of working. Some routes for promotion for an installer are increasingly skilled jobs such as PBX repairer, supervisor, and sales or customer service person.

Although installers must work accurately and efficiently at all times and especially in emergencies, Mary Ellen Mathews finds her job exceptionally gratifying.

"I find it very satisfying to walk out of a house where I've done the job from beginning to end. After I test a phone and hear it work I feel great! There aren't many opportunities where you get to do this," she says.

To be an installer you need the interest and ability to be a skilled technical worker who not only enjoys meeting the public, but can also work independently. Your occupation is needed wherever there are telephones, which is just about everywhere.

For more information, contact the unions to which most telephone workers belong:

- Communications Workers of America
  1925 K Street, NW
  Washington DC 20006
- International Brotherhood of Electrical Workers
  1125 15th Street, NW
  Washington, DC 20005
- Telecommunications International Union
  2341 Whitney Avenue
  Hamden, CT 06518

Chapter **IV**

Television

Both television and radio are vital to American society, not only for entertainment, but also for information and education. Production of programs from broadcasting stations, located throughout the country, usually goes on twenty-four hours a day. Women have slowly increased their numbers in the nontraditional jobs in this industry, most of which are in the engineering and production departments of stations.

Opportunities for highly competitive entry jobs exist in small stations. Job openings are expected to increase as cable stations and in-house closed-circuit facilities grow.

BROADCAST TECHNICIAN

Even while Renee Butler was still in high school, she knew she wanted to be part of the television industry. Her ambition was to be a broadcast technician, a job requiring knowledge of electronics to operate and maintain equipment for recording and transmitting television and radio programs. Unlike many of her friends, Renee had no doubts about not choosing the more traditional occupations for women. Instead, she zeroed in on her goal by taking appropriate training after high school and by applying for summer internships with a TV station.

"Because there aren't many women in technician's jobs, men supervisors are unwilling to hire and train women. You need assertiveness and persistence to land an internship if you want this valuable experience," she cautions.

Her own perseverance helped her find an internship with an educational TV station, where her co-workers and supervisor

RENEE BUTLER, BROADCAST TECHNICIAN.

were impressed by her enthusiasm, willingness to learn, and capabilities. In spite of strong competition, when she finished her education she was hired by the station as an apprentice broadcast technician.

For those who want to be in an occupation that's indispensable to the operation of a TV studio, investigating this work should be very rewarding. However, you need the kind of personality that thrives on pressure to meet deadlines. Also, while the work is not physically strenuous, you may have to stand for long periods of time while repairing or adjusting equipment. In addition, you need:

- good vision, color perception, and hearing;
- above-average manual dexterity and touch discrimination;
- excellent ability to concentrate in spite of chaotic conditions around you.

Before career training there are several ways you could measure your own motivation and abilities for a future in this field:

- Take as much math as you can in high school, including geometry and trigonometry, as well as science and shop courses.
- Join clubs or take school courses where you can participate in actual production of TV programs.
- Apply for a summer or part-time job in a TV or radio station.
- Build electronic hobby kits such as stereo sets.

Ideally you should begin preparation for this job in high school by planning your program to meet entrance requirements for post–high school training. Courses for a technician's career are offered at technical or trade schools, community colleges (two years), and colleges (four years).

Each year organizations such as the National Association of Broadcasters, local TV stations, and other industry groups award scholarships and financial help to those who want to study to become technicians. Ask your guidance counselor about eligibility for these scholarships and financial assistance.

Most technicians are graduates of two-year post–high school programs. The curricula usually include:

- fundamentals of direct and alternating currents,
- technical drafting,
- technical mathematics,
- electronic principles,

- circuitry,
- trigonometry,
- calculus,
- television broadcast theory and practice,
- television workshops,
- communication skills,
- psychology of human relations,
- computer programming for technicians.

For a list of schools offering these courses, contact:

- Broadcast Education Association
  1771 N Street, NW
  Washington, DC 20036
- American Women in Radio and Television Inc.
  1321 Connecticut Avenue, NW
  Washington, DC 20036

After completing your training you can begin your job hunt by using several resources for that entry-level job:

- Apply directly to the chief engineer or personnel manager of a TV station.
- Obtain help from the placement office of your school.
- Write to these two national organizations. The first is committed to helping minorities and women find jobs in broadcasting. Both services are free:
- National Association of Broadcasters Employment Clearinghouse
  1771 N Street NW
  Washington, DC 20036
- PACT, National Association of Educational Broadcasters
  1346 Connecticut Avenue, NW
  Washington, DC 20036

Jobs for broadcast technicians exist not only in commercial and educational TV stations, but also in growing public and private sectors such as:

- hospital audiovisual centers,

- school radio and television closed-circuit systems,
- government agency studios,
- commercial film production houses,
- industry closed-circuit television systems.

Your best prospects for a beginner's job is in the TV station of a small city, where they're willing to hire someone inexperienced. In smaller stations you'll perform many technical functions all within one day's shift. You'll gain varied, excellent experience. But first, as a new technician, you'll begin the job with a period of instruction from the chief or senior engineer. Each station has its own procedures that you'll have to learn and follow. You'll also find that the titles "technician," "operator," and "engineer" are used interchangeably.

In the studio some of your duties are likely to be:

- setting up lights, microphones, and cameras;
- operating a control room console to select pictures and sound that go on the air, switching from camera to camera or from studio to recorded video or audio material;
- using hand signals to give technical directions to studio personnel.

Occasionally you'll work outside the studio broadcasting sports, news, or an interview. Your duties might be:

- unloading and setting up equipment,
- locating a telephone transmission link to the studio,
- setting up a microwave transmitter and testing equipment and transmission before broadcasting.

In smaller stations, technicians work at a variety of jobs, but in the larger city stations they are employed in various specialized positions. A sampling of these are:

- Videotape recording operator: operates and maintains videotape equipment to transcribe live programs.
- Video engineer: operates the control panel of video consoles; sets switches and observes readings to control contrast, brightness, quality, and size of television picture.

- Audio engineer: regulates volume and quality of sound by adjusting controls.
- Microphone boom operator: positions microphones to pick up performers' voices without interfering with studio lighting.
- Transmitter engineer: operates and maintains television transmitters according to regulations of the Federal Communications Commission; monitors incoming and outgoing signals to assure strength, clarity, and reliability.

Since 1981 the Federal Communications Commission (FCC) requires any technician who operates, installs, and maintains transmitting equipment to have "any class" radiotelephone operator's license. Most broadcast technicians apply for a restricted license (a "753"), issued without examination for the life of the holder. But technicians who work with microwave or internal radio communication equipment must have a general radiotelephone operator's license. To get one, you must pass a series of exams given by the FCC covering basic communications and electronics. Community colleges and technical schools give courses to prepare for these tests. The FCC schedules exams twice a week, and no fee is required.

A technician's daily routine offers constantly varying subject matter as well as opportunities for new challenges and experiences. Among the advantages of the job are the following:

- Salary: entry-level salaries in the 1980s were about $16,000 per year based on a 40-hour week. Overtime is common and is paid at time-and-a-half. In urban areas, technicians earn ⅔ more than those in smaller rural stations. Educational stations pay less than commercial stations.
- Conditions: technicians work in pleasant, well-lighted, air-conditioned surroundings.
- Fringe benefits: benefits vary in small stations. Most large stations have health insurance, paid sick leave, paid holidays, and vacation programs.

Since TV stations operate twenty-four hours a day, seven days a week, a technician may have to work inconvenient shifts, holidays, and weekends, which can be a drawback. Other possible disadvantages:

- tension and strain caused by making split-second decisions for which the technician alone is responsible;
- long unscheduled hours of work during emergencies;
- severe weather and uncomfortable locations when broadcasting outside the studio.

Although Renee Butler's colleagues in this male-dominated occupation have been cooperative and helpful, many women have had more negative experiences. They've found resistance to the hiring, training, and promoting of women. For this reason Women in Broadcasting was founded. The organization supports women who want to enter the better-paying nontraditional jobs by giving advice, encouragement, and information. It offers service not only to beginners, but also to those who want to advance in the industry.

Technicians who gain the necessary experience and show above-average ability and leadership can advance to higher positions. The route is usually from a small station to a larger one that has more supervisory jobs and higher salaries. Promotion possibilities are to supervisor, technical director, chief engineer (usually requires a degree in electrical or electronic engineering), or manager of technical operations (also may require a degree in engineering).

Although broadcast technicians work in every state, the majority are in metropolitan areas where the specialized jobs are concentrated. The need for technicians is expected to grow about as fast as the average for all occupations through the mid-1990s. Opportunities will arise as new stations go on the air, established stations increase their hours, and cable TV stations originate more of their own programs. Moreover, private and government groups are expected to expand the television medium as a communication and educational tool.

As a broadcast technician you would have the satisfaction of being part of a staff that copes with complex, sometimes hectic problems to run a television station with expertise, efficiency, and reliability. You'll find a need for your skills throughout the country, and as you grow in experience you'll enjoy substantial salary increases and promotion opportunities.

For more information, contact:

- National Association of Broadcast Employees and Technicians
  7101 Wisconsin Avenue
  Washington, DC 20014
- Institute of Electrical and Electronic Engineers
  345 East 47th Street
  New York, NY 10017
- Federal Communications Commission
  1919 M Street, NW
  Washington, DC 20554

CAMERA OPERATOR

As an ENG (electronic news gathering) camera operator for a public TV station, Eileen Layman is never sure what her workday will bring. She may be shooting a chemical fire, a political interview, or a traffic accident. Recording dangers, disasters, and calamities is a daily activity for her. She's part of a news team that's out in the field gathering material to meet a 6:30 p.m. program deadline. Her shift, scheduled for eight hours, may last much longer, depending on extraordinary or unexpected events. Even though her team's crew chief is the reporter, Eileen contributes her ideas for shooting extra footage to improve the story.

Although she held clerical jobs while completing her education in communications, Eileen Layman always intended to work in the TV industry. Her first job was as an audio-control technician, accompanying the reporter and camera operator on assignments. Her duties were to direct the microphone to speakers and maintain the volume and quality of the sound. Occasionally she had opportunities to do some shooting assignments. As a result, she gradually acquired enough experience to become a full-fledged ENG camera operator. Her camera weighs 40 pounds, and her battery belt (powering the camera) another 5 pounds. She's accustomed to carrying this equipment, but after a 10-hour day, she says, "It starts getting heavy."

Ms. Layman advises women who want to enter this field that the work is hard, the competition intense, but the job is immensely rewarding and well worth pursuing.

EILEEN LAYMAN, CAMERA OPERATOR.

"You need plenty of drive and tenacity to get what you want," she says.

To be a camera operator you need training, but even before taking courses, you should be aware of the special aptitudes and qualities required for this occupation:

- Creativity to find new, interesting, and imaginative ways of shooting a subject; a strong sense of picture composition.
- Responsiveness to orders with speed and agility, whether in the studio or on location.
- Physical stamina to stand as well as carry equipment; portable cameras, however, are getting lighter and smaller, making location work easier.
- Communication skills, both verbal and written, so that you can quickly explain your ideas, as well as understand your co-workers.
- Vision, color perception, and hearing need to be excellent; spatial perception and good eye-hand coordination are also necessary.
- Concentration to complete your duties even while distracting and confusing activities are all around you.

Some ways you could explore your interest in this vocation before devoting yourself to more extensive career training are to:

- take courses in high school in English, speech, math, physics, and TV production;
- join clubs or hobby groups where you can participate in TV production; if you're lucky enough to have access to a video camera, practice shooting;
- apply for a summer or part-time position as a helper in a TV studio.

Since camera operators need training, you'll require a special program if you decide on this vocation. First, have your high school diploma or its equivalent. Then you'll have a choice of schools offering appropriate classes, such as: vocational school, technical institute, two-year community college, four-year college, or a continuing education program in college or university.

To find schools convenient to you, check your library for

directories such as *Lovejoy's* or *Barron's* for listings of colleges. Write to the organizations listed below for free brochures giving listings of additional schools:

- American Women in Radio and Television, Inc.
  1321 Connecticut Avenue, NW
  Washington, DC 20036
- National Association of Trade and Technical Schools
  2251 Wisconsin Avenue, NW
  Washington, DC 20007
- Broadcast Education Association
  1771 N Street, NW
  Washington, DC 20036

At whatever school you choose, ask the guidance counselor or admissions officer about financial help, particularly for women interested in nontraditional jobs. In this industry professional organizations frequently offer scholarships.

You'll find some of your subjects will be:

- introduction to video tape,
- lighting for video and film,
- videotape workshop,
- documentary video,
- cable TV production,
- commercial TV production.

When you've completed your program, your school placement office will be one source of help in locating a job. However, you'll find your search more productive if you're prepared to accept employment in a small station in a suburban or rural area. These smaller facilities are more likely to hire inexperienced beginners. Also, they offer varied responsibilities and more chances to gain wider experience and skills than the highly demanding, specialized urban stations.

Other organizations that may help you are:

- National Association of Broadcasters Employment
  Clearinghouse
  1771 N Street, NW

Washington, DC 20036
(this group is committed to helping women and minorities find jobs in commercial broadcasting)
- PACT, National Association of Educational Broadcasters
  1346 Connecticut Avenue, NW
  Washington, DC 20036

You can also apply directly to the personnel departments of TV stations. Furthermore, since camera operators work in many establishments other than TV stations, you could apply to the audiovisual studios of hospitals, government agencies, schools, businesses, and commercial film production houses.

You may be hired immediately as a camera operator or, like Eileen Layman, start in another capacity such as production assistant or technician. Once on the job you'll usually be part of the engineering department and report to the engineering supervisor. In some stations camera operators are members of the production department and are supervised by the production manager.

Most stations have at least two camera operators on staff. One may be assigned to the news department and take orders from the news director. In the studio the operator receives her instructions via a headset from a director or a technical director.

Duties of the camera operator include altering angles and distances by camera placement and manipulation of the camera lens, and maintaining sharp focus and good framing.

The ENG operator has the same technical responsibilities as the studio operator, and she responds rapidly to instructions from the reporter. She can also suggest added taping for background material.

In addition, camera operators in some studios, particularly smaller ones, may assist:

- the audio/video engineer in the setup, technical check, and simple maintenance of television cameras;
- the lighting director in setting up scenery, lighting equipment, and other properties before a production;
- the floor manager or unit manager in dismantling a production.

Furthermore, most camera operators need a Federal Communications Commission (FCC) license to work. Technical schools and community colleges offer courses to prepare for FCC licensing tests. The agency gives these exams twice a week, and there is no fee.

In addition to the exciting variety and challenges that are part of this job, camera operators also have other advantages.

- Salary: may range from $400 to $800 per week, depending on experience, location, and union. Urban stations pay more than rural stations; commercial stations pay more than public TV.
- Hours: 40 hours, 5-day-week, 8-hour shifts; overtime is paid at time-and-one-half.
- Conditions: most camera operators work in air-conditioned, well-lighted, pleasant studios.
- Fringe benefits: smaller stations have varying benefits; large stations offer health insurance, paid holidays, sick leave, and vacations.

Disadvantages include:

- pressure: meeting deadlines with exacting work can cause tension and anxiety;
- hazards: on location there can be exposure to danger before unpredictable situations are under control such as in fires, explosions, or shooting incidents;
- severe weather: outside the studio the camera operator may have to work in all kinds of rough weather;
- shift work: odd hours may cause inconvenience and disruption of routines;
- emergency calls: camera operators may have to be on duty during long, unscheduled hours.

Women in this vocation have increased their employment numbers somewhat slowly. Though Eileen Layman is the only woman camera operator in her station, she has not experienced any harassment from men co-workers. She also points out, however, that her duties aren't made easier for her because she's a woman; she's expected to handle her own work. American

Women in Radio and Television is a support group for women in the industry and encourages women to enter the better-paying nontraditional jobs. You can write to them for more information.

Chances for advancement in this career are good, especially for those who continue their education and gain experience. Camera operators can move up to floor manager, lighting director, or audio/video engineer.

Camera operators are needed in every state. In spite of competition for openings, new positions will be available as independent and cable stations expand production and education, government, business, and health institutions increasingly use the TV medium.

Women who want to be a crucial part of a television team will find particular satisfaction in this work. After gaining experience in a small station, they can generally move up to the larger stations, earning higher wages, better fringe benefits, and promotions.

For more information, write to:

- National Association of Broadcast Employees and Technicians, AFL-CIO (NABET)
  7101 Wisconsin Avenue
  Washington, DC 20014
- Federal Communications Commission
  1919 M Street, NW
  Washington, DC 20554

Chapter **V**

Transportation

Transportation is a major American industry, moving people and goods. Increasing numbers of women, in nontraditional jobs both in operation and maintenance, are working in every branch of this field. Some areas of transportation are railroads, ships, aircraft, and trucks and buses. For the future, air and highway jobs are expected to increase. However, railroad and maritime jobs are expected to decline.

BUS DRIVER

A sense of humor and an easygoing personality are what you need to succeed as a bus driver, according to Alice Shiffrin. She ought to know because she's a local transit bus driver herself, who recommends the occupation to women who want to make "a decent living." However, you need to like both driving and dealing with people.

After graduating from high school, Alice tried work as a typist, cashier, and factory assembler. Besides finding that she didn't like being indoors, she also discovered that she couldn't earn enough to cover her expenses. But among her various jobs, she'd been a part-time school bus driver. Realizing that she liked driving and enjoyed being responsible for a busload of passengers, she started searching for a full-time bus driver's job. In a newspaper help-wanted column she saw an advertisement for drivers, and she eagerly tried for the job. The position, held almost exclusively by men, was opened to women by this company. Alice Shiffrin applied, was evaluated, and was hired.

After her training she began her routine as a new driver and was

ALICE SHIFFRIN, BUS DRIVER.

placed on the same shift system as other new employees. She has a job she enjoys and that pays her well.

Though driving a bus isn't physically strenuous, you do need some special qualifications, such as good eye, foot, and hand coordination, quick reflexes, and good depth perception.

Since most transit companies require a driver to be at least 21 years old, there's ample time to investigate your own interest in the occupation. You can take driver education courses in high school, then obtain your driver's license and apply for jobs, part or full time, as a school bus driver, taxi driver, or delivery driver.

If you need a chauffeur's license, call the state Motor Vehicle Department for requirements. You'll probably be scheduled for a driving test, a written test of your knowledge of traffic regulations, and a physical exam. You need to have at least 20/40 vision without glasses and to be in good health.

If you have the basic requirements and want help in finding a bus driver's job:

- Contact bus companies directly by calling their personnel offices and asking for an application and appointment. Look in the telephone yellow pages under Bus Lines.
- Ask the state employment service for a referral to a job.
- Look for newspaper help-wanted ads.

Most transit companies give screening tests to prospective employees. You'll probably be asked to take a physical. In addition to 20/40 vision, good hearing, and normal use of legs and arms, you need general good health. You may be given a written exam to evaluate your ability to read and write job-related materials such as schedules, notices, labels, and reports.

If you are hired, you'll be given a training program lasting from two to eight weeks, both in the classroom and out driving. Classroom subjects include:

- company work rules,
- safety regulations,
- state and municipal driving regulations,
- schedule reading,
- fare determination,
- record-keeping.

Driving training offers:

- zigzag practice,
- backing up,
- driving in narrow lanes,
- driving on lightly traveled roads,
- driving on heavily congested highways,
- trial runs without passengers to learn routes.

Future bus drivers learn defensive driving because they're seated higher than other drivers, permitting them to see farther ahead. From their position they can spot traffic dangers and avoid them. After completing training, new drivers take final written and driving exams. If they pass they begin the job with a "break-in period." During this time they make regularly scheduled trips with passengers, accompanied by an experienced driver who will give helpful tips, answer questions, and assess the new driver's performance.

Like Alice Shiffrin, local transit bus drivers provide public transportation within a metropolitan area. Intercity drivers operate buses between any size community and a metropolitan area. Both kinds of drivers have the same routine in starting their workday. Drivers report to their assigned terminal or garage and then:

- collect tickets, transfers, refund, and trip report forms;
- check tires, brakes, windshield wipers, lights, oil, fuel, and water;
- make certain safety equipment such as fire extinguishers, first-aid kits, and emergency reflectors are on board;
- drive to the start of the run.

Once out on her run, the local bus driver must:

- make regular stops according to her route and time schedule;
- collect fares, tokens, tickets, or transfers;
- change money where exact fare isn't offered;
- check student or senior identification cards;
- answer questions regarding schedules, routes, transfer points, and street numbers;
- enforce safety rules and regulations of the company and the city;
- regulate heating, air conditioning, or lights on the bus;
- prepare and turn in a trip sheet including records of fares, trips made, and any delays or accidents.

An intercity driver who is in complete charge of her bus must:

- supervise the loading of baggage;
- pick up passengers at terminals or designated places;
- collect fares;
- drive at speeds that keep established time schedules;
- discharge passengers at special stops;
- make regular stops for meals, and check the return to the bus of all passengers;

- supervise unloading of passengers and baggage at destination;
- prepare reports on mileage, fares, and time as required by the company and the Interstate Commerce Commission;
- write a complete account of any accident or unusual delay during the run.

Among the reasons women like Alice Shiffrin have been eager to become bus drivers are the advantages enjoyed by these workers. Here is a sampling:

- Wages: *local bus drivers* earned an average of $12.50 per hour for the journeyperson level in the mid-1980s; usually drivers are paid hourly in agreements worked out by unions and management; salaries may depend on size of the city, length of service, and type of run: *intercity bus drivers* earned an average of $25,000 per year for an experienced driver in the mid-1980s.
- Hours: *local drivers* have a 40-hour, 5-day workweek with time and a half for overtime; five consecutive work days may include Saturdays and Sundays, which are considered regular workdays; some companies operate 24 hours a day and drivers have to rotate shifts; *intercity bus drivers* have a 32- to 36-hour workweek; drivers may not work more than 10 consecutive hours without at least 8 hours off; drivers are limited to 60 hours on duty in a 7-day period.
- Fringe benefits: both types of drivers have life and health insurance, pension plans, paid vacations, holidays, and sick leave.
- Conditions: for those who like their independence, drivers work without direct supervision and assume responsibility for the way they do their work.

Although there are disadvantages in the job, Alice Shiffrin says that the positive aspects outweigh any problems she encounters. Nevertheless, you should consider them too:

- weekend and holiday work;
- night shifts;

- tension from driving a large vehicle on congested streets and from dealing with many types of people;
- pressure from the need to keep on schedule;
- hazards from driving in bad weather;
- emergency duty on short notice because drivers are always on call;
- layoff for those with little seniority when business declines.

Women applying for bus-driving jobs and those in training may experience skeptical attitudes and even hostility from supervisors, trainers, and some men co-workers. Alice Shiffrin and the other women drivers in her company have received cooperation and support from both administration and colleagues, but not all women have been that lucky. You should be aware that you may meet opposition and prejudice on the job.

For most bus drivers, advancement usually means better assignments and higher earnings as their seniority increases. However, there are also promotion opportunities to dispatcher, supervisor, sales representative, instructor, terminal manager, or regional manager.

Local bus drivers looking for work in both the immediate and the long-range future will find openings occurring at about the average for all jobs. There will be some new jobs and opportunities to fill vacanies left by drivers who retire or leave for other reasons. Some factors that can improve the long-range outlook for local transit drivers are federal legislation to improve all forms of local public transportation, and cities' efforts to attract people to downtown shopping areas by offering convenient local public transportation.

Employment for intercity bus drivers is expected to be slower than the average for all occupations through the 1990s. Fewer bus drivers will be needed because more people will be using planes that offer cheap fares, enabling them to travel faster over longer distances.

Those women who have steady nerves and enjoy driving and working without supervision can look to bus driving as a career with several advantages. Good salaries, fringe benefits, and feelings of pride for assuming responsibility for the safety and comfort of passengers are part of the job. In addition, bus drivers work in every state, though mainly in metropolitan areas. For more information, write to:

- American Public Transportation Association
  1225 Connecticut Avenue, NW
  Washington, DC 20036
- Transport Workers Union of America
  1980 Broadway
  New York, NY 10023
- American Bus Association
  1025 Connecticut Avenue, NW
  Washington, DC 20036

LOCAL TRUCK DRIVER

Sometimes a negative experience can change your life. That happened to Bonnie Billings. Disappointment with working as a veterinarian's assistant prompted her to change careers, choosing instead a job as a local truck driver for a national parcel delivery company. After graduation from a community college with an applied science degree, she pursued a career as a veterinarian's assistant, but she found that the work meant low salary, lack of fringe benefits, and long unpaid extra hours. Although she liked working with animals, she needed a higher salary, and when the delivery company opened its high-paying driving jobs to women, she decided to apply. Since she had driven an ice cream truck on summer vacations, she was already an experienced driver. It was work she knew and liked, and after passing the company's physical and driving tests, she was hired.

Nowadays, wearing the company uniform, she picks up or delivers parcels weighing up to 50 pounds. She enjoys the physical activity because, she says, "It keeps me in shape."

Although there are many satisfying conditions about her job, the ones she especially likes are being outdoors and working independently. "I don't like someone telling me what to do," she says. "In this job I'm on my own, I know what to do, and I can handle everything."

She also points out that her salary has risen higher than those of her friends working as veterinary assistants, clerks, or teachers. As

BONNIE BILLINGS, LOCAL TRUCK DRIVER.

a member of a Teamsters Union local, she enjoys "decent" fringe benefits negotiated by the union. If you're independent, like driving, and can do the heavy lifting, carrying, and walking, you'll want to look into driving a local truck. However, there are some traits all drivers need:

- Calmness under pressure: You may drive in terrible weather, traffic tie-ups and other unexpected situations; nevertheless, you'll be expected to meet your delivery schedule.
- Decisiveness: You have to be able to think quickly and decisively to get things back to routine as soon as possible.
- Responsibility: Because you're on your own, you have to be conscientious, reliable, and self-motivated to fulfill your duties.

Even though there is no long training period for this job, you can determine your own interest in local truck driving before applying for an actual job by:

- taking a high school driver-training course as well as classes in automotive mechanics;
- applying for a summer job as a driver's helper or temporary relief driver;
- studying truck driving at a technical or vocational school. Completing the course doesn't guarantee a job. Check with a local trucking company before enrolling to make sure the school's training is acceptable to them.

You need a chauffeur's license for this occupation. Call the state Motor Vehicle Bureau for details. Usually they give these qualifying tests:

- A general physical examination including vision; you need 20/40 sight without glasses.
- A written examination on driving regulations.
- A driving test.

Although driving is not physically demanding because of comfortable seats, good ventilation, and improved cab design, drivers should be in good health because they have to lift heavy objects. Preference is also given to applicants with:

- good driving record;
- some previous experience driving a truck, including in the armed forces, or as a trucker's helper;
- neat appearance and ability to speak well; some drivers deal directly with customers and must get along with the public.

You can get help in hunting for a truck driver's job from several sources:

- state employment service;
- local trucking firms: look in the yellow pages under Trucking;
- newspaper help-wanted advertisements.

Though you may not land a full-time driving job immediately, you can start as a substitute driver when regulars are out sick or on vacation, an extra driver during heavy seasonal demand, or a driver's helper.

You'll find, after you're hired, that your training is likely to be both informal and brief. New drivers may get a few hours of instruction by riding with and observing a veteran driver. Then you begin your own run. If you're driving an unusual type of truck, your company will furnish additional training. Some companies give one or two days of classroom training covering general duties, operation and loading of a truck, company policies, and preparation of delivery forms and company records. If you're hired as a driver–sales worker you'll receive training on the company's products.

Although there is great variety in companies employing local truck drivers, all require the driver to follow these routines:

- Start the run by receiving assignments from the dispatcher to determine whether she'll be making deliveries, pickups, or both.
- Check her truck for fuel, oil, and proper functioning of brakes, windshield wipers, and lights.
- See that fire extinguishers, flares, and other safety equipment are aboard.
- Adjust mirrors so that both sides of the truck are visible from the driver's seat.
- Select forms and other paperwork necessary for the day's

run; customers must sign receipts for goods, and drivers (sometimes bonded) receive money for materials and need records of these transactions.
- Make sure cargo has been loaded properly so it won't shift during the trip.

Drivers report to the dispatcher any equipment that doesn't work or is missing and cargo that is improperly loaded.

Once on the road the driver has to maneuver her vehicle skillfully through congested streets without accidents. She also must be able to pull into tight parking spaces, negotiate narrow alleys, and back up to loading platforms.

Other work done by a local truck driver depends on the product or service she deals with. Some examples are:

- Produce trucker: picks up a loaded truck in the morning and spends the day delivering the produce to stores.
- Lumber trucker: makes several trips from the lumberyard to one or more construction sites.
- Gasoline tank truck driver: attaches hoses and operates pumps on her truck to transfer gasoline to gas station storage tanks.

Drivers having sales and customer-relations responsibilities are called route drivers or driver–sales workers. They deliver their firm's products but also represent the company. How they handle customers can make the difference in building or losing business. Successful route drivers use sales ability to increase sales and gain new customers.

Duties of driver–sales workers vary according to their industry and the policies of their company, and how strongly their sales responsibility is emphasized. Most have wholesale routes. Some examples are:

- Wholesale bakery driver–sales worker: delivers and arranges bread, cakes, rolls on display racks of markets. By paying attention to goods on the shelves, she can estimate amount of baked goods that will be sold. She may recommend changes in a store's order or may encourage the manager to stock new

products. Occasionally she may try to get the business of new stores along her route.
- Laundry driver–sales worker: rents linens, towels, work clothes, and similar items; visits businesses regularly to replace soiled laundry.
- Vending machine driver–sales worker: services machines in factories, schools, and other buildings; checks stock remaining in the machines; replaces stock and removes money and deposits it in cash boxes. She also examines each vending machine to see that merchandise and change are dispensed properly, makes minor repairs, and cleans machines.

Many local truck drivers like Bonnie Billings are members of the International Brotherhood of Teamsters, Chauffeurs, Warehousemen and Helpers of America. Occasionally truckers are members of unions that represent the company's plant workers. Some advantages drivers enjoy are:

- Salary: $10 per hour was the average in the mid-1980s, but this varies widely according to area, size of truck, kind of product, and local union; some driver–sales workers receive commissions based on sales.
- Hours: 40-hour week with extra pay for overtime.
- Fringe benefits: health and insurance coverage, pension plans, paid holidays, and vacations.
- Uniforms: where necessary, supplied by the employer.

In spite of the benefits, driving in this industry has disadvantages, such as hazards, of driving in storms, snow, and all kinds of severe weather; nerve-wracking traffic; and pressure to meet delivery schedules.

Though local truck drivers work in even the smallest towns, most jobs are located in and around metropolitan areas. However, because of the growth of suburban shopping centers, freight deliveries will increase, and that means more employment for drivers. Moreover, there will be openings throughout the country to replace drivers who retire, transfer, or change jobs. Therefore, the employment outlook for local drivers is expected to increase through the 1990s.

Some slowdown in employment may occur for driver–sales

workers. The trend has been to replace these truckers with sales and office staffs. Drivers may be confined to delivery duties only.

A local truck driver can look forward to advancement depending on seniority, experience, and competence. Some opportunities are as dispatcher, supervisor, terminal manager, traffic manager, or long-distance truck driver (trailer truck driver).

Although Bonnie Billings did not encounter resistance from her company in hiring women, you may find opposition when you apply for this work. The occupation has been dominated by men, and personnel managers or supervisors may be skeptical about hiring a woman as a local truck driver. Once on the job you may also encounter some hostility from customers and co-workers.

But for a woman who is in good health and doesn't object to the heavy lifting, this job can offer decided benefits. You can work outdoors independently, and since local truck driving has one of the largest number of job openings each year, you can easily find work in any part of the country with a good salary, hours, and fringe benefits.

For more information, write to:

- American Trucking Association, Inc.
  1616 P Street, NW
  Washington, DC 20036

Chapter **VI**

Mechanics, Repairers, and Related Occupations

One of the fastest-growing categories of skilled workers in our country is that of mechanics who repair and maintain our machines. Throughout the 1980s the need for their services will increase, and since unemployment is usually low for such occupations, these jobs will offer a stable livelihood. In addition, women are finding entry into a wide variety of industries that use mechanics and repairers.

Industries offering the largest numbers of job openings are:

- automotive,
- appliances and machinery,
- airlines,
- communications.

AIR CONDITIONING, REFRIGERATION, AND HEATING MECHANIC

Can you imagine your supermaket or favorite restaurant without refrigeration? For that matter, what would you think about businesses and homes without heat in winter, air conditioning in summer, and refrigeration all the time? Avis Thompson is a trainee mechanic in the industry that keeps these cooling and heating systems operating and in good repair.

Although she had always wanted to work in a skilled trade, Ms. Thompson never had the chance until she enrolled in a women's outreach center, which helps women enter nontraditional trades. After evaluation and counseling, Avis Thompson asked for training as an air-conditioning mechanic. A special grant enabled the center to place her in a trade school, where she enrolled in an intensive six-month program at no cost to herself. After she had finished her course, the school furnished her with a set of tools and helped her find a job in a shop that repairs and maintains commercial air conditioners. She is learning to repair fans, compressors, and condensers and becoming familiar with many special tools used in this trade.

Training for becoming a mechanic in this skilled trade involves three to four years as an apprentice or an on-the-job trainee. Therefore, you need to consider some of the requirements before you commit yourself to it. As a mechanic you need:

- excellent physical health: considerable lifting and moving of heavy equipment is necessary; also mechanics may work in awkward, cramped positions;
- normal eyesight and good color perception;
- above-average mechanical aptitude and manual dexterity, including eye-hand coordination and spatial perception;
- responsible, dependable personality: willingness and capacity to learn new, intricate tasks; ability to work accurately and precisely without supervision.

Although most employers or contractors are reluctant to hire inexperienced and untrained helpers in this trade, you may still find some opportunities for exploration by:

- visiting a repair shop or a trade or technical school to observe and ask questions about the nature and conditions of the work;
- taking courses in high school in physics, math, mechanical drawing, and metal and wood shop;
- enrolling in a women's outreach center for testing and counseling. Although funding for some women's centers may cease, new organizations may become available; for help in finding a center near you, contact the YWCA, the Women's Bureau, U.S. Department of Labor, or the state employment service.

Although there are several routes to learning this trade, most employers want an applicant to have a high school diploma. In addition, they prefer to hire beginners who have taken courses in air conditioning, refrigeration, and heating. Completing such a program makes you more employable because you won't need as much on-the-job training. You can find courses in a public or private community college or a technical or vocational school. To find the nearest one write to:

- Air Conditioning and Refrigeration Institute
  1815 North Fort Meyer Drive
  Arlington, VA 22209

Some of the classes you would take in post–high school training are:

- air-conditioning theory;
- heating theory;
- refrigeration theory;
- design and construction of equipment;
- basics of installation, maintenance, and repair of heating, refrigeration, and air-conditioning equipment.

After finishing your course work you can get help in finding an entry job by:

- asking your school placement office for a referral;
- checking the help-wanted ads in newspapers;
- registering with the state employment service;
- applying directly to employers: look in the telephone yellow pages under Air-Conditioning Contractors, Heating Contractors, and Refrigeration Servicing.

On your first job you'll be assigned simple tasks, and as you progress your level of skill will do so too. As a trainee you will:

- carry materials,
- insulate refrigerant lines,
- clean furnaces,

- cut and solder pipes and sheet metal,
- check electrical circuits.

Another highly desirable way to learn this trade, especially in unionized areas, is through a formal four-year apprenticeship. These programs are operated jointly by the locals of the United Association of the Plumbing and Pipefitting Industry and the Associated Builders and Contractors. To find such an apprenticeship, write or call:

- Bureau of Apprenticeship Training, U.S. Department of Labor;
- Apprenticeship Council, State Department of Labor;
- Apprenticeship Committee of a local of the United Association of the Plumbing and Pipefitting Industry.

As part of the application process for apprenticeship, a committee made up of union members and employers will screen and test you for:

- education,
- mechanical aptitude and manual dexterity,
- physical health,
- previous employment.

If you obtain an apprenticeship, you receive on-the-job training supplemented by 144 hours each year of classroom instruction in such subjects as safety practices, care of tools, blueprint reading, and air-conditioning theory.

Whether you learn your craft in a formal apprenticeship or as an on-the-job trainee, your work will be to install, maintain, and repair air-conditioning, heating, and refrigeration systems. You need to know the operating machinery as well as the connecting ducts and pipes.

Mechanics often specialize in a particular category such as air conditioning and refrigeration. The duties of the mechanic in this specialty are:

- installation: following blueprints, design specifications, or

manufacturer's recommendations, install motors, compressors, condensing units and evaporators; connect this equipment to ducts, refrigerant lines, and electrical power sources; charge the system with refrigerant; check for proper operation;
- malfunctions and maintenance: diagnose breakdown causes by testing compressors, relays, and thermostats; make necessary repairs; overhaul compressors and inspect system for any required maintenance.

In another category, heating mechanics, also called furnace installers, do some of the following:

- install oil, gas, electric, solid fuel, and multifuel heating systems by following blueprints or specifications;
- connect furnace to fuel supply lines, air ducts, pumps, and electrical wiring and controls;
- check the furnace for proper operation.

Besides installation, in fall and winter the heating mechanics frequently service and adjust oil burners. They may:

- check the thermostat, burner nozzles, oil and air filters, ducts, and vents;
- adjust or replace inoperative or inefficient parts.

Gas burner or gas appliance mechanics perform similar tasks to those servicing oil burners. They may:

- locate and repair malfunctions in gas-fueled heating systems;
- inspect and clean heating systems in preparation for the next heating season;
- repair other gas appliances: cooking stoves, clothes dryers, hot water heaters, outdoor grills.

Regardless of specialty, the mechanic in this trade needs certain tools. In addition to the customary ones such as hammers, wrenches, and pliers, she'll use metal snips, pipe cutters and benders, acetylene torch, and electric drill.

For testing and checking electrical circuits, burners, and other components, she'll use measuring devices including gauges, manometers, and volt-ohmmeters.

Even though mechanics finish training, they never stop learning. Changes and advances in technology require them to keep up to date. They do so by taking courses offered by various professional associations, for example:

- Refrigeration Service
   Engineers Society
- Petroleum Marketing
   Education Foundation
- Air Conditioning
   Contractors of America

Though their duties are complicated and demanding, workers in this industry enjoy numerous benefits:

- Earnings: experienced mechanics earn $17 to $26 per hour; for overtime the rate is time-and-a-half; these rates vary according to locality, union, and type of shop or business.
- Hours: 40-hour, 5-day workweek is customary; during peak seasons overtime and irregular hours are common; there may be layoffs or reduced hours when the season is over; shops servicing both air-conditioning and heating equipment operate all year.
- Fringe benefits: paid vacations and holidays, sick leave, medical and life insurance, retirement plans.

There are, of course, disadvantages to be considered:

- Working conditions: may be at heights or in dirty, noisy, oily factory areas.
- Pressure: in emergencies you may have to work quickly under tension.
- Hazards: cuts from tools, electric shocks or burns, injuries from chemicals or moving machine parts; good safety procedures lessen these dangers.

As the only woman in her shop, Avis Thompson feels lucky because her men co-workers are cooperative and helpful. She feels she contributed to the relaxed atmosphere by demonstrating that she can handle her fair share of duties needing heavy lifting or job expertise. However, women in other shops have met with resentment, and you should be prepared for skepticism not only in your own shop but on the customer's premises.

For experienced mechanics, particularly those who get along well with people and have good judgment and planning skills, advancement is possible to lead mechanic, supervisor, estimator, city or county inspector, or manufacturer's service specialist.

Although being a mechanic in this industry is hard work and requires training of three to four years, the investment and effort may be well worthwhile. Job openings are expected to increase faster than the average for all other occupations through the 1990s. Some reasons for the favorable job outlook are demands for climate-control systems in new commercial and residential construction, renovation of systems in existing buildings, and replacement of mechanics who leave, transfer, or retire from the trade.

Another bonus of this craft is that it is not sensitive to economic fluctuations. Since businesses depend on air conditioning, heating, and refrigeration, there will always be a need for mechanics to do the maintenance and repair. Servicing and modernizing of existing systems make up a large part of the mechanic's work.

Mechanics work in all parts of the country. Oil burner specialists are concentrated in the Northeast where oil is a major fuel.

Women willing to train for this highly skilled, physically demanding work will have careers with excellent wages and fringe benefits. Furthermore, they can look forward to a good supply of future job openings throughout the country.

For more information, contact:

- Air Conditioning Contractors of America
  1228 17th Street, NW
  Washington, DC 20005
- Refrigeration Service Engineers Society
  1666 Rand Road
  Des Plaines, IL 60016
- Petroleum Marketing Education Foundation
  P.O. Box 11187
  Columbia, SC 29211

AIRCRAFT MECHANIC

Sandra Matos, a talented, skilled aircraft mechanic, has always had a deep commitment to a career in aviation. She began working toward her objective when she was a teenager by attending a vocational high school specializing in aviation mechanics. After graduating, she enrolled for another year in a trade school approved by the Federal Aviation Administration (FAA) for more courses to sharpen and expand her knowledge.

Currently, Sandra works as a mechanic for a large independent overhaul shop. She holds two FAA licenses, the airframe and the powerplant. The first permits her to service and repair any part of the outer frame of a plane. The second, the powerplant license, allows her to maintain and repair engines. During her workweek she is likely to be busy dismantling an engine, replacing worn or defective parts of landing gear, or splicing wire or cable. Her duties are varied, and she has many different assignments depending on the needs of the shop.

To help her stay agile and strong so that she can do the heavy lifting, bending, and crouching necessary for a mechanic, Sandra works out in a gym and at home. Her efforts, she feels, are very worthwhile because she's in a vocation that offers her so much satisfaction.

"Maybe," she says, "working around greasy, oily machine parts and tools wouldn't be considered glamorous, but I feel an inner glamour when I see a plane I've worked on taking off and flying."

If you'd like to be a part of this exciting, complex, yet rigorous industry, you can measure your own interest and abilities before you complete high school or start advanced post–high school training:

- Take math, physics, mechanical drawing and automechanics, and electrical and metal shop courses in high school.
- Repair, experiment, and tinker with automobile engines.
- Assemble and fly model airplanes.
- Find a part-time or summer job as a helper at an airfield or airport.
- Enroll in a women's outreach center (usually at the YWCA) for courses in the use of hand tools or repairing of electrical devices.

SANDRA MATOS, AIRCRAFT MECHANIC.

MECHANICS, REPAIRERS, AND RELATED OCCUPATIONS

Although years ago mechanics were able to learn their craft by on-the-job training, this is rarely possible today. Nowadays, most mechanics learn their job in the armed forces or in FAA-certified schools. Before attending a school, you need to consider some requirements of the aircraft mechanic:

- Physical: above-average strength to lift heavy parts and tools; agility for climbing, often on scaffolds, ladders, and on the plane; stamina to work in awkward positions such as crouching, stooping, and kneeling.
- Exceptional mechanical aptitude and manual dexterity.
- Good vision and color discrimination.
- Strong sense of responsibility to complete work thoroughly, accurately, and precisely; capacity to work with others on a team.

If you decide you want to enter this industry, you need a high school diploma. Beyond high school you need to find an aircraft mechanic program in an FAA-certified trade school. Write to the FAA for an up-to-date list of schools:

- Director of FAA Certified Aviation Maintenance Technician Schools (AC147-2)
  Publications Section, M-443.1
  U.S. Department of Transportation
  Washington, DC 20590

Your trade school will provide you with tools and equipment; courses usually last from 18 months to two years. After completing the program you'll be eligible to take the FAA licensing exams as an airframe mechanic, a powerplant mechanic, or both. The exams consist of a written test, an oral test, and a demonstration of ability to do the work authorized by the license. The trade school, however, can't guarantee the FAA license, or even that you'll get a job.

Finding that first, or entry, job may require you to relocate to another community. There is less competition for jobs in smaller companies located in rural and suburban areas. You can get help in finding a job from:

- placement service of your trade school,
- personnel office of individual airlines,
- state employment service.

Many different facilities employ aircraft mechanics:

- Airports: line mechanics work at airports making emergency and other necessary repairs after aircraft land and before they take off.
- Airline overhaul bases: base mechanics perform major repairs and periodic inspections on aircraft.
- Independent aircraft overhaul and repair bases: mechanics here do the same work as in airline bases, but not for only one company.
- Flying schools.
- Private firms that own and operate their own planes.
- Aircraft manufacturing plants.
- U.S. Air Force and Navy bases that employ civilian mechanics.

No matter what the workplace, as an airframe mechanic your duties would include inspecting, servicing, and repairing parts of the plane such as wings, fuselage, fuel tanks, control devices, and propeller devices.

To correct problems and malfunctions, some of your tasks would be to:

- visually inspect all parts of the frame for signs of rust, cracks, or distortions;
- replace sheet metal surface areas;
- measure tension of control cables;
- replace worn or defective assemblies.

As a powerplant mechanic you'd work on various types of engines, including radial, turbojet, turboprop, and rocket.

The duties of the powerplant mechanic are to:

- inspect external appearance of the engine for cracked cylinders, oil leaks or cracks, and breaks in the turbine blades;

- listen to the engine to detect sticking or burnt valves;
- remove engine (if necessary) with hoist, and take engine apart; use sensitive instruments (such as x-ray) to check for invisible cracks;
- replace or repair worn or damaged parts;
- reassemble and reinstall the engine.

In performing their work, mechanics use a large assortment of hand and power tools, including power shears, sheet metal breakers, acetylene welding equipment, rivet guns, air or electric drills, wrenches, screwdrivers, and pliers.

Although in smaller companies mechanics make many kinds of repairs, some commercial airlines use specialized mechanics for systems such as electrical, navigational, communication, and hydraulic.

Regardless of the specialty, a mechanic in this industry enjoys several advantages:

- Earnings: $17 an hour, plus shift and longevity pay; wages vary, depending on type of company, union contract, and location.
- Hours: 40 hours, 8 hours per day, 5 days a week; shifts are scheduled around the clock.
- Conditions: work is usually performed in well-lit, airy hangars and maintenance shops; occasionally line mechanics work outdoors in bad weather.
- Fringe benefits: paid vacations and holidays; health and life insurance; paid sick leave; retirement plans.
- Reduced air fares: mechanics and their immediate families receive a limited amount of free or reduced air fares on their own and other companies' flights.

Disadvantages in this field are from:

- pressure: mechanics often have to work quickly yet accurately to keep from inconveniencing customers and disrupting schedules;
- hazards: falls from heights while working on large jet planes;
- noise: testing of engines causes vibration and noise that can damage ears; use of special ear covers curtails this problem;

- dangers: poisoning from inhalation of fumes from carbon monoxide, gas, or paint; burns from hot engines or flammable fluids; cuts from tools or machine parts;
- layoffs: during recessions, airlines cut the number of flights, reducing the need for mechanics.

Sandra Matos says that women who want to become aircraft mechanics need to be persevering and assertive. They meet with skepticism not only from supervisors but from instructors, causing problems in both learning and working. She and other women mechanics must constantly demonstrate that they can perform their duties physically and technically. This situation can be an additional source of tension and pressure in a shop, and women should take it into account. However, Sandra observes that women are overcoming prejudice as they prove themselves capable mechanics.

"Some of the women have moved on to bigger firms with better-paying jobs, and some have been promoted to supervisory positions," she says.

For most mechanics, working conditions are determined by their union. The majority of mechanics belong to the Air Transport Division of the Transport Workers Union of America. Other unions covering mechanics are the Aircraft Mechanics Fraternal Association and the International Brotherhood of Teamsters, Chauffeurs, Warehousemen, and Helpers of America.

Advancement or promotion for a mechanic usually depends on length of experience and competence. Both of these elements can be enhanced by constantly updating skills. Since new technologies are always evolving, the mechanic should attend industry seminars, manufacturers' informational meetings, and special shop or factory courses.

Adding to her qualifications by keeping up with new developments and by taking other FAA licenses, a mechanic can move up to head mechanic or crew chief, aircraft inspector, shop supervisor, or engineering, administrative, or executive positions; the last-named usually require additional training.

In the last half of the 1980s, the general aviation industry expects to have an increase in mechanic's job openings because of growth of business, with more planes flying passengers and freight; and vacancies because of job changes, transfers, or retirements.

MECHANICS, REPAIRERS, AND RELATED OCCUPATIONS

The number of jobs for mechanics employed by the federal government is expected to stay the same but may be affected by whether the defense budget is increased or reduced.

The aviation industry depends on its highly skilled aircraft mechanics, and if you're a woman interested in being part of it, you'll have a demanding, well-paying job with excellent fringe benefits. In addition, you'll have opportunities to work for a variety of establishments throughout the country.

For more information, write to:

- Aviation Maintenance Foundation Inc.
  P.O. Box 739
  Basin, WY 82410
- Air Transport Association of America
  1709 New York Avenue, NW
  Washington, DC 20006
  (This organization will send you a list of airline companies and their addresses.)

AUTO MECHANIC

"I like it because it's challenging and it's interesting," says Esther Clark, auto mechanic for a large national chain of stores. "The challenge comes from successfully finishing a repair job and seeing a very doubtful customer leave happy and satisfied. The work is never routine and the variety holds my interest."

Always enthusiastic and curious about tinkering with cars, Esther Clark decided to take a free auto repair course at the local YWCA. This Y, like many throughout the country, had an outreach program that encouraged women to explore trades. She learned the basic parts of an automobile engine and found that, despite the ever-present grease, grime, and oil, she enjoyed auto mechanics. After the six-week exploratory course, the Y offered the graduates a list of large companies willing to hire apprentice auto mechanics.

Although in the past the field of auto mechanics was largely limited to men, affirmative action programs administered by both federal and state governments have changed that situation. Today, businesses are required to recruit women and other minority groups for apprenticeship programs. Esther Clark was able to

ESTHER CLARK, AUTO MECHANIC

obtain such an apprenticeship by applying directly to the personnel office of a national company. She has been receiving on-the-job training in the various departments of the auto shop. As she learned each new skill, she was advanced to more complicated work. A salary raise accompanied each advancement.

"Dull, and with no real future," Esther Clark says of the jobs she had previously held as a telephone operator and a clerical worker. She also took a two-year college course in radiology, but found she didn't like either the work or the conditions involved. Now her salary is higher than those of most of her friends in either secretarial or radiology jobs, and she expects to earn more as she becomes more skilled.

Just what are the duties of an auto mechanic? A thoroughly trained and experienced auto mechanic's most important task and valuable skill is to make a quick and accurate diagnosis of a car's mechanical problem. Naturally, this takes training (about four years as an apprentice) and good reasoning ability.

The experienced mechanic begins by asking the car owner for a description of the problem. From there the mechanic uses increasingly sophisticated machines to reveal what malfunction exists in the auto being tested. Some of this equipment may be:

- oscilloscope, a device that shows on a screen changes in voltage;
- dynamometer, a power-measuring device used to check engine efficiency without removing the engine from the car;
- computer the electronic machine that processes the data and produces answers to the problems.

After reading the material furnished by these electronic machines, the mechanic can show the customer a printout or computer report indicating where the breakdown has occurred and what repairs are necessary.

Once the problem is known, the mechanic must repair or replace the car's defective part. In repairing or rebuilding the part, the mechanic may have to use power or hand tools. Power tools, driven by electric motors, are used when the volume of work or the labor saved is sufficient to warrant the cost. A few of them are:

- welding and flame cutting equipment for cutting stock or joining metal parts;

- pneumatic wrench for removing or installing bolts, nuts, and studs;
- milling machine for cutting gears and slots, sawing metal, finishing flat surfaces;
- lathe for turning stock while it is being machined;
- shapers and planers to shape or reduce the size of a metal part;
- grinding machine for removing metal with an abrasive wheel.

Use of power tools requires proper training. Also, because these tools sometimes throw off chips or sparks, mechanics must wear safety goggles to avoid accident and injury.

A great variety of hand tools are needed by the mechanic, and within each category are many types and sizes, depending on use. Here are a few:

- hammers and mallets, shaped heads attached to handles, used to bend metal, join or separate;
- pliers, pincer-like instrument with long jaws that have teeth for gripping; used for cutting, bending, and tightening nuts or bolts;
- screwdriver, single blade in a handle for loosening or tightening slotted screws;
- chisel, rod-like tool with a cutting edge at one end; used for cutting or chipping metal;
- wrench, open-end box for loosening or tightening nuts and bolts;
- file, hardened steel tool for removing, smoothing, or polishing metal.

These are just a few of the tools ranging from simple to the more complicated and expensive that the mechanic uses. Some mechanics furnish their own hand tools, and an experienced mechanic may invest hundreds of dollars in her equipment.

While most mechanics can perform a wide variety of repairs, it's also possible to specialize. Specialists may work in large shops with several departments or in small shops that concentrate on one particular product. Some specialties are:

- brake mechanic: works on hydraulic and power brake systems;

- automatic transmission mechanic: works on gear trains, couplings, hydraulic pumps, and other parts of automatic transmissions;
- front end mechanic: concerned with suspension and steering systems;
- electrical repair mechanic: adjusts, repairs, and installs voltage regulators, generators, and any other parts of the ignition system;
- body and fender mechanic: removes dents in the auto body; replaces any body sections requiring new sheet metal, glass, or trim.

Because of the complexity of the automobile, other specialties require both basic auto mechanic skills and specialized training. In addition, automobile mechanics must keep up to date on new developments by reading service and repair manuals, shop bulletins, and other technical publications as well as attending special courses.

But whether the mechanic is general or specialized, she usually works in a shop that may be partially open. This may mean that in winter the area will be cold, and in summer hot. Grease, dirt, sparks, and noise are constant factors in the auto shop environment. Lifting of heavy auto parts and tools is sometimes necessary, as well as working in awkward positions. Minor cuts and bruises are common in this trade, but good safety practices prevent serious accidents.

Women may find that special problems exist for them in the shop. Not only may their men co-workers be hostile toward them, but their customers, both men and women, may also be suspicious and unwilling to allow women to repair their cars. Esther Clark observed a change in her co-workers' attitudes when they learned that the women mechanics were competent. Her customers were gratified when she and other women mechanics satisfactorily completed their repair jobs. However, in some shops acceptance of women is reluctant or absent. This can mean a continual atmosphere of strain, especially for women apprentices.

For women who wish to qualify as automobile mechanics the best route is apprenticeship. Today's vehicles are so complex that "pick-up" education, trying to learn by working in small garages picking up information informally, is insufficient. The apprenticeship is a four-year systematic plan with on-the-job training and 140 hours of formal classroom instruction each year. This program is operated jointly by the local labor union and the employers' association. In this industry, however, the would-be apprentice should apply to the state employment agency for an apprentice's application and exam. The examination tests knowledge of English; knowledge of mathematics and basic science; and mechanical aptitude.

If the candidate passes the exam, the joint committee evaluates her qualifications, including:

- education: a high school diploma or the GED is required;
- trade or vocational courses: this can be an outreach women's program or private vocational school courses; high school subjects such as math, science, and shop are also significant;
- previous work history: any related work such as gas station attendant is relevant;
- physical condition: you should be in good health and able to do heavy lifting, bending, and crouching.

The joint committee is responsible for the systematic planning and overseeing of the on-the-job training as well as the subject matter in the classroom. The pay for an apprentice is 60 percent of the journeyperson's wages at the beginning, with regular raises. The state employment service or the joint committee helps place the apprentice in a job.

To find your state employment agency check the white pages of the telephone book under the name of your state; look for the heading Employment Department or Bureau. The yellow pages under Labor Unions or Associations will give you the names of the local auto worker's unions. Some of them are:

- International Association of Machinists, Aerospace, and Agricultural Implement Workers of America
- United Automobile, Aerospace, and Agricultural Implement Workers of America
- International Brotherhood of Teamsters, Chauffeurs, Warehousemen and Helpers of America

Future prospects for automobile mechanics are so promising

that the training necessary for this career appears to be an excellent investment. Employment demands are expected to grow faster for these mechanics than the average for all other occupations in the 1980s. Mechanics will be needed because of the expanding population reaching driving age, increasing dependence on the auto for transportation, and the growing complexity of auto devices requiring maintenance. In the early 1980s the average hourly wage for auto mechanics was $10.32. Naturally this varies at different times and in different localities throughout the country. Another positive factor for auto mechanics is that they can find jobs anywhere in the U.S.—if not the world.

In addition to allowing the mechanic to be very mobile, this industry offers good advancement possibilities. Some of them are to lead mechanic, repair supervisor estimator, or service manager.

Following are several employers' associations to which you can write for guidance and data:

- Automotive Service Industry Association
  444 North Michigan Avenue
  Chicago, Illinois
- Automotive Service Councils, Inc.
  188 Industrial Drive
  Elmhurst, IL 60126
- National Automobile Dealers Association
  8400 Westpark Drive
  McLean, VA 22102

BOILER TENDER

Making sure the tenants in 1,200 apartments have heat and hot water is a responsibility that Doris Welsh, a boiler tender, proudly assumes. She works for a city housing authority as a member of the heating plant technical staff, helping to maintain the low-pressure boilers that deliver those vital utilities. Under supervision, she dispenses chemical treatments for water, checks meters and gauges for proper oil and water temperature, and maintains and repairs pipes, vacuum pumps, and other equipment. During her work shift she uses a variety of hand tools such as wrenches, pliers, and screwdrivers.

For Doris Welsh, who worked for twelve years as a secretary, her present job is a vast improvement, and not only because of her higher salary.

"I don't have to be stuck in one place, just typing. Now I meet all kinds of people, get a chance to do responsible work, and I can advance. I don't mind the dirty fingernails. The job is getting more mechanized with computers and becoming easier," she says.

Although the housing authority management did not actively encourage women, when this position was opened to everyone Doris decided to apply. At no cost, applicants could enroll for a year in an evening program for jobs as boiler tenders. Those successfully completing the course could look forward to employment in a city housing complex.

Before acceptance, applicants were screened for their capabilities and suitability for the training. They took tests for knowledge of math and for mechanical aptitude and manual dexterity. In addition, a high school diploma or its equivalent was required.

Although boiler tenders may have to work in shifts around the clock, as Doris does, she feels that her salary, fringe benefits, and promotion opportunities more than compensate for odd hours. She has the same attitude about the dirt, grease, and oil present at her workplace.

Probably the best way to measure your own interest in being a boiler tender would be to find a summer or part-time job as a boiler room helper. You can also:

- take math, chemistry, and wood or metal shop in high school;
- take courses in heating or ventilation in a vocational or trade school;
- enroll in a women's outreach center for courses in the use of hand tools; the YWCA can help you locate a center.

Since most equipment used for heating today is mechanized, boiler tenders don't need unusual physical strength. However, they do need good vision and hearing and ability to stand, walk, crouch, and kneel for long periods of time.

Most employers provide on-the-job training to those without experience, but high school graduates are preferred. To succeed as a trainee you need mechanical aptitude and dexterity so that you can learn how machinery works and how to use tools to make repairs. For help in finding an entry job in this occupation you can consult:

- personnel or employment offices of establishments using boiler tenders such as hospitals, apartment house complexes, office buildings, factories;
- state employment service;
- help-wanted ads in newspapers.

As a new employee you start as a helper, working under the supervision of an experienced boiler tender or the stationary engineer. As you become more skilled, you gradually undertake more responsible duties. Some tasks of the boiler tender are to:

- inspect boiler equipment;
- light the boiler and build up steam pressure;
- read meters and gauges, adjusting controls as required;
- make minor repairs on the equipment;
- add chemicals to the boiler to prevent corrosion and scale;
- use mechanical devices to control the flow of air, gas, oil, or powdered coal into the firebox of the boiler.

To make sure the boilers are operating properly and in conformity with safety regulations, the boiler tender uses meters and other measuring and safety devices. An experienced boiler tender can sometimes detect trouble by listening to the machinery as she adjusts and inspects the controls.

In some cities and states boiler tenders are required to be licensed. A new employee may start as a helper and then operate under a conditional license, but eventually she must obtain a license for high-pressure boilers, low-pressure boilers, or both.

Allowing for some variations, most licensing exams include a written test and an evaluation of experience considering length of time and duties.

With either license, a boiler tender can work on most of the equipment as long as a stationary engineer is on duty to supervise.

This occupation offers several advantages:

- Earnings: $8.15 per hour in the mid-1980s; these rates vary in different industries as well as localities.

- Hours: 8-hour day, 40-hour week; shifts, weekend, and holiday work where boiler rooms operate 24 hours a day.
- Fringe benefits: paid holidays, vacations, hospitalization, medical insurance, retirement pensions.

Although many boiler rooms are clean and well lighted, some are not. Furthermore, besides clutter and dirt in your environment, there may be other disadvantages such as:

- noise and heat from the machinery;
- fumes from oil, gas, or coal;
- discomfort from working in awkward positions; occasionally workers have to crawl into the boilers for inspection and repair;
- danger from burns, falls, or electric shock; good safety procedures lessen these hazards.

Though Doris Welsh and her women co-workers represent a very small percentage of the maintenance staff in her workplace, she finds that women in nontraditional jobs have become better accepted.

"We were hassled at first by men who weren't used to women doing the same job," she observes.

But after proving themselves competent, the women have met with much less resistance. Doris recommends that women in nontraditional jobs contact other women with similar problems for support and advice. Though women are being accepted into the ranks of boiler tenders, you may still meet prejudice when you apply for such a job. To find a women's support group try contacting:

- National Organization for Women
- YWCA
- Women's Bureau, U.S. Department of Labor

With expertise and skill gained from experience, a boiler tender can look for promotion to supervisor or to jobs requiring the experience but more formal training: maintenance mechanic and stationary engineer.

The need for boiler tenders is expected to be steady through the mid-1990s. In spite of increased mechanization, there will be job openings to replace workers who leave the industry, retire, or transfer to other jobs.

In this occupation the more skills you acquire from experience, special training, or related courses, the better your chances for job security. You can advance yourself by enrolling in:

- trade or vocational schools;
- community, technical, or junior colleges;
- accredited correspondence schools.

Boiler tenders work in every state, though most are employed in heavily populated areas with large industrial and commercial buildings. For women who want better-paying, more interesting work, Doris Welsh recommends this job. She also suggests that women look beyond "dirty fingernails" to the variety, challenge, and opportunities to advance to more skilled positions.

For more information, contact:

- International Brotherhood of Fireman and Oilers
  200 Maryland Avenue, NW
  Washington, DC 20002
- International Union of Operating Engineers
  1125 17th Street, NW
  Washington, DC 20036

BUILDING CUSTODIAN

Laverne Lun, a building custodian, firmly believes that women should learn to do as much as possible for themselves to become independent and self-sufficient. Because of these convictions, she started on the road to her present career. First, at an adult center in a technical high school, she took courses in paperhanging and painting. After mastering those skills, she branched out to home plumbing and electrical repairs. But she felt that the high school center gave too much theory and not enough hands-on practice, so she enrolled in an evening continuing-education program in a technical community college. Here, women who wanted to qualify for nontraditional jobs received training and special attention.

LAVERNE LUN, BUILDING CUSTODIAN.

In the school's Apartment House Institute, Ms. Lun took subjects such as:

- Renovation Management
- Basic Plumbing Repairs in Housing
- Basic Electrical Maintenance
- Energy Efficiency Training
- Burner/Boiler Operation for Superintendents
- The Apartment House Physical Plant
- Refrigeration Mechanics

In her classes, she also gained expertise in the use of hand and power tools. After six months she completed a program requiring 200 hours of coursework.

From other women in her classes Ms. Lun heard about a job as a building custodian for an organization that offered home repair services to elderly people living in a rundown section of the city. The organization was pleased to hire her because their clients felt safer and more comfortable admitting a woman to their homes. Laverne began a job doing work she says she "loves." Her hours are flexible, her duties constantly changing, and her salary is higher than on her former job.

What Laverne left behind was a job as an executive secretary for a publishing company. She had always felt that sitting in an office all day was confining, uninteresting, and monotonous. In her present occupation she's using her abilities to help people who need her special knowledge, and the challenges she meets give her a satisfaction in her work that was missing in former jobs.

Although Laverne doesn't go beyond the surface of walls, the range of her repair and maintenance tasks is very diverse. She may:

- repair a bell,
- fix fan controls,
- plaster a hole in the wall,
- fix a ceiling light,
- modify a drain in a bathroom sink,
- snake the drain in the kitchen,
- tighten a faucet in the kitchen,
- unblock a toilet.

Another source of gratification for her has been the opportunity to teach a course in home repair and maintenance at the technical community college where she originally took her own training. She passes along her skills in a program called "Women Teaching Women."

If the special project for the homebound elderly that employs her should lose funding, Laverne is confident that she can move to another job. She would apply for positions as either a supervisor or a manager in private building or public housing management.

To determine your own interest in becoming a building custodian you can try several methods:

- take high school shop courses in carpentry and metal;
- enroll in home repair courses in an adult continuing-education center;
- find a part-time or summer job as a helper to a building custodian;
- check courses in the use of hand tools at a women's outreach center. The YWCA may have such a center, or can refer you to one.

Service custodians are on their feet most of the day. For this job you need to be able to walk and stand for long periods of time. In addition, you should be able to lift heavy objects, bend, stoop, kneel, and crouch. Some other special requirements are:

- ability to treat people courteously and tactfully. Custodians often have to deal with complaints and requests from tenants living or working in the building;
- capacity to plan duties and work without direct supervision; dependability and reliability are important because you need to follow through on your duties.

Women who want jobs in this field should have a high school diploma or its equivalent. Courses in housing maintenance and repair will add to your qualifications and employability. Both public and private post–high school facilities have special programs for women interested in nontraditional job training. Telephone your school and ask the guidance counselor or admissions officer for information. You can look for this valuable training (sometimes given free or at low cost) in:

- public community, junior, or technical colleges;
- private technical and vocational schools; for a national directory of accredited private schools, write to the National Association of Trade and Technical Schools, 2021 K Street NW, Washington, DC 20006;
- unions: the Service Employees International Union offers courses in cities throughout the country. Look in the telephone yellow pages under Labor Associations for the local nearest you.

Whether you're in a community college or a technical or vocational school, you'll cover subject areas such as:

- safety and health regulations;
- operation and maintenance of machines such as vacuums, buffers, and polishers;
- repair and maintenance of electrical, plumbing, and refrigeration equipment;
- building and housing carpentry;
- repair and maintenance of heating and air-conditioning systems.

Though building custodians are needed throughout the country, most work in towns and cities. They work in a wide variety of establishments, including schools, hotels, hospitals, apartment houses, office buildings, and factories.

After completing your training you can get help in locating that first job by:

- asking for a job referral from the state employment service;
- checking help-wanted ads in the newspapers;
- applying to the managers of buildings;
- applying at janitorial service companies; look in the telephone yellow pages under Office Cleaning.

Once on the job you may be the only custodian or part of a staff. Your duties very likely will include:

- fixing leaky faucets and making other minor plumbing repairs;
- painting and carpentry;
- making minor repairs on refrigeration and air-conditioning systems;
- vacuuming carpets;
- washing and waxing floors with electric machines or mops;
- disposing of trash;
- replacing lights and fuses and making minor electrical repairs;
- polishing metal fixtures;
- mowing lawns or shoveling snow.

Since custodians work independently, they can usually adapt their activities to their own schedules and work at their own pace. This occupation has other advantages:

- Salary: unionized custodians earn $10 an hour; nonunion firms pay from $6 to $8 an hour; wages depend on locality, size of business, and type of industry.
- Hours: 40-hour week, 8-hour day, but in buildings open 24 hours custodians may have to work shifts; some custodians prefer night work;
- Fringe benefits: most building custodians receive paid holidays, vacations, and health insurance.

The drawbacks in this work are from:

- hazards from falls from ladders, or on wet floors or icy sidewalks;
- exposure to harsh cleaning materials;
- minor cuts and bruises from power machines and hand tools.

Laverne recommends this job for women who want flexible hours and enjoy making repairs. Since building custodians have usually been men, she says that many specialized repair men she's hired have met her with "wonder." She predicts that although women may meet with resistance and some hostility in finding and keeping jobs, time and patience will help assimilate them into this field. She also suggests that women join a network to meet other women in the trades. You can get help in finding such groups by calling:

- National Organization for Women
- YWCA
- Women's Bureau, U.S. Department of Labor

The future for new jobs for building custodians is favorable. There will be an increase in the number of openings throughout the 1980s because of increases in new building and the general affluence of the population demanding service.

With experience, building custodians can look forward to advancement to several positions such as supervisor, manager, or independent maintenance contractor.

If you're a woman in good physical shape and can work with tools and power machines, and with tenants, you can earn a good living as a building custodian. You'll certainly rarely find yourself bored!

For more information, contact the union most building custodians join:

- Service Employees International Union
  2020 K Street, NW
  Washington, DC 20006

ELECTRONICS TECHNICIAN

Probably one of the most exciting, important industries in the United States, both today and in the foreseeable future, is electronics. Computers show the biggest growth, but hosts of new consumer and industrial products are being developed in this technological explosion. Just a small sampling of products the industry has provided are videotape and disc recorders, microwave ovens, telecommunication equipment, commercial measuring and control devices, and navigational instruments.

Even foreign competition, changes in economic conditions, and cuts in government spending will not cause a serious decline in the growth potential of this field or its need for trained technicians.

Arlene Crosby is just such a technician who recently received an Associate of Applied Science degree in electronics at a technical

ARLENE CROSBY, ELECTRONICS TECHNICIAN.

institute. Her school placement department helped her find her first job, where she assists in the production and manufacture of electronic measuring devices.

Although Arlene has always done mechanical work such as factory assembling and radio and television repairing, she recognized the need for more education to enter a better-paying, more secure career. After enrolling in a four-year college, she switched to a two-year technical institute where she was able to earn a degree and concentrate on career training.

Arlene says that most of her friends are employed in various clerical occupations. She is proud that she studied electronics and challenged the stereotyping of women into narrow job categories. In addition, she's delighted with her salary and looks forward to a higher-paying and very rewarding future in this rapidly growing field.

The work of electronics technicians is essential to the development, manufacture, modification, and maintenance of components and equipment. Regardless of the specialty or phase of product development, the general duties of technicians include:

- setting up apparatus;
- conducting tests;
- analyzing tests;
- preparing reports, sketches, graphs, and schematic drawings to describe electronic systems.

If you see yourself as a future electronics technician, you need certain aptitudes and qualities, such as:

- ability to do neat, detailed, accurate, and methodical work;
- sufficient initiative, responsibility, and independence to perform without close supervision;
- competent communication skills, both written and verbal;
- mechanical aptitude and manual dexterity;
- normal eyesight and color perception;
- strong interest and aptitude in math, science, and electronics.

Most of the duties of the technician are not physically strenuous, and you don't need unusual strength. You may have to do some standing, walking, and occasional lifting.

Knowing some of the requirements, you can evaluate yourself and measure your motivation for this occupation. To learn more you could:

- take high school courses in algebra, geometry, physics, shop, and mechanical drawing;
- enroll in vocational or trade school for courses in basic electricity or electronics;
- contact women's outreach centers and study electrical repair or use of hand tools; inquire at the YWCA or state employment service to find a center;
- join electronics or radio clubs and participate in assembling electronic equipment with commercial kits;
- ask your school guidance counselor to arrange visits to research laboratories, service shops, or manufacturing plants to gain realistic knowledge about the industry.

You'll need a high school diploma or the equivalent if you decide to enter this career. The preferred way to enter is to take a two-year training program. You can find listings of schools by checking these directories in your library:

- *Lovejoy's Career and Vocational School Guide*
- *Barron's Guide to the Two-Year Colleges* (Vol. 2)
- *Peterson's Annual Guide to Undergraduate Study*

For a free booklet of trade and technical schools you can write to:

- National Association of Trade and Technical Schools
  2021 K Street, NW
  Washington, DC 20006

Many types of institutions offer courses in electronics. When you decide on a school, check with the guidance counselor for scholarships and for any special financial help for women interested in nontraditional job training. Several types of training establishments are:

- technical institutes,

MECHANICS, REPAIRERS, AND RELATED OCCUPATIONS 109

- junior and community colleges,
- extension divisions of colleges and universities,
- public and private vocational schools,
- armed forces.

In your first year some typical courses might be:

- physics for electronics,
- technical math,
- electronic devices,
- circuit analysis, AC and DC,
- instruments and measurements,
- communication skills.

In your second year you'll probably study:

- communication circuits,
- introduction to digital electronics,
- technical reporting,
- drawing, sketching, and diagramming,
- communications systems,
- electronic design and fabrication,
- introduction to new electronic devices.

When you have completed your program, the school placement department can help you find a job. Other resources for finding an entry position are:

- state employment service;
- help-wanted ads in newspapers;
- electronics companies: consult the telephone yellow pages under Electronic Research and Development or Electronic Instruments.

Chances are that you'll find employment in one of the three broad areas of electronics, and your duties will vary accordingly. The first category is product development. Mainly, these technicians:

- build, test, and modify models of new electronic products;

- make verbal or written reports for improvement of a device;
- construct, install, modify, or repair laboratory test equipment;
- convert rough sketches and written and verbal information into schematic layouts or wiring diagrams;
- estimate costs of manufacturing a new product.

A second division is manufacturing and production. Some tasks of these electronic technicians may be to:

- maintain complex automated machines used to build the electronic product;
- train or supervise production teams in testing or building a product.

In the quality and control category, technicians:

- inspect and test the product at various stages of production;
- maintain and calibrate test equipment used in the manufacturing process;
- determine causes for rejection of parts or equipment by the assembly-line inspectors;
- analyze reports of product failures;
- submit reports for elimination of rejects;
- suggest design, manufacturing, and process changes.

To work effectively, technicians consult manuals and other reference materials. They also use many tools and complex equipment such as:

- computers,
- calculators,
- drafting tools,
- bench lathes,
- hand tools: drills, pliers, wrenches, screwdrivers, files, hammers;
- voltmeters;
- oscilloscopes;
- signal generators;
- electronic frequency counters.

Electronics offers its technicians several advantages:

- Wages: $15 an hour or over, depending on experience, knowledge, particular shop, and geographic location.
- Hours: 40 hours per week, 5 days, Monday to Friday; for shifts there is usually a 10 to 15% pay premium; overtime is paid at time and one half, double time for holidays.
- Fringe benefits: paid vacations and sick leave; all major holidays; health and life insurance; some employers offer profit-sharing and stock purchase plans and bonus programs.
- Conditions: most technicians work in modern, comfortable, well-lighted surroundings; injuries are infrequent and not likely to be serious.

Technicians may have to deal with drawbacks such as:

- shift work: may cause inconvenience because of odd hours;
- hazards: occasional exposure to electrical shocks from equipment.

Although women who want to train and find jobs as technicians may find resistance from instructors and supervisors, many are overcoming these obstacles. Arlene Crosby found cooperation from her male co-workers in her shop. However, women may need to prove themselves capable before they're fully accepted as trainees or journeyperson technicians.

Those who acquire experience and are interested in advancing will need to continue their vocational growth with further education. Science and engineering are continually presenting changes, and technicians need to keep up with new challenges and information. A competent, knowledgeable technician can look for promotion to supervisor, senior technician, engineering assistant, production test supervisor, or quality assurance supervisor.

Conditions of work for technicians in manufacturing plants may depend on their particular union. Some of the unions they belong to are:

- International Union of Electrical Radio and Machine Workers
- International Brotherhood of Electrical Workers

- International Association of Machinists and Aerospace Workers
- United Electrical, Radio and Machine Workers of America

For the future electronic technicians will have little difficulty in finding jobs. Predictions are that this industry will grow substantially over the next decade. Moreover, the need for technicians is expected to increase much faster than the average for all other jobs because of increased demand for computers, communication equipment, military electronics, and electronic consumer goods.

Women who enjoy math and science and are willing to develop their potential with special training can find exceptional rewards as electronic technicians. They'll be part of an expanding industry that offers excellent salaries, promotions, fringe benefits, and employment throughout the country.

For more information, contact:

- The Electronics Industries Association
  2001 I Street
  Washington, DC 20006
- Accreditation Board of Engineering
  345 East 47th Street
  New York, NY 10017
- International Society of Certified Electronics Technicians
  2708 W. Berry
  Ft. Worth, TX 76109
- American Electronics Association
  2680 Hanover Street
  Palo Alto, CA 94304
- Electronics Technicians Association International, R.R. 3
  Box 564
  Greencastle, IN 46135

LOCKSMITH

Rescuing drivers locked out of their cars, repairing bank safes, and changing home locks are all in a day's work for April Truitt. She's a locksmith whose varied and unusual days mean installing, fixing, and readjusting locks for almost any kind of business or

MECHANICS, REPAIRERS, AND RELATED OCCUPATIONS 113

APRIL TRUITT, LOCKSMITH.

residence in what she describes as "creative" and "satisfying" work. She's been a locksmith for the past eight years and in her company van outfitted with tools and equipment she's prepared for anything from the ordinary to the unexpected. Even though her regular working hours are 8 to 4, Monday to Friday, she's always available to handle frantic emergency calls at any time, day or night.

Back when April was pumping gas on a part-time job while in school, she was interested in mechanical work. Her original goal was to be an auto mechanic, and she took as many shop courses as she could. After graduation she applied for an apprenticeship for the mechanic's job, and while waiting she answered a newspaper ad for an office job in a locksmith's shop. Although her first duties were to answer the telephone, take care of the office, and do some light bench work, she soon learned most of the locksmith's tasks in the shop. She abandoned her ambition to be an auto mechanic and, like most locksmiths, continued her training with informal on-the-job situations. By changing jobs several times, she was able to gain wider experience and knowledge in most aspects of the craft. Supplementing her on-the-job training, she took special courses offered by industry associations. Her goal these days is to specialize in bank safes and electronic security systems.

You may find it helpful to explore the field before committing yourself to a full-time job if this vocation interests you. Here are some ways you can do so:

- find a part-time or summer job as a helper to a locksmith;
- take wood and metal shop, math, and drafting in high school;
- enroll in a private vocational or trade school for blueprint reading, welding, and mechanical designing;
- contact a women's outreach center (try the YWCA) for a course in using hand tools.

Locksmithing requires several diverse qualities:

- patience to do detailed work with precision and accuracy;
- good vision and spatial perception;
- eye-hand coordination and above-average manual dexterity;
- capacity to understand written and oral instructions;
- honesty, dependability, reliability;

- ability to work without close supervision and to get along with people;
- good health to cope with considerable standing, bending and stooping, and some heavy lifting;
- good driving record.

Another prerequisite for a job in this trade is eligibility to be bonded. Many employers will not hire a trainee who cannot meet the bonding company's requirements for this type of insurance. Having anything but a very minor police record could be a serious barrier to working as a locksmith.

Since there is no formal apprenticeship in this industry, you can make yourself more employable by attending a locksmith school or taking a correspondence course. You can write or telephone the Associated Locksmiths of America for a list of schools. Look in the telephone white pages for the branch nearest you.

If you decide to apply for a trainee job, you should be at least 18 years old and have a high school diploma or the GED. You can check these resources for help in finding your first job:

- state employment service;
- newspaper ads for helper or trainee;
- locksmiths in your vicinity; you can apply directly by calling and asking for an appointment for a job interview.

On the job you can improve your skills by further training such as learning about electronics, building codes, and sales techniques. You can find courses in these subjects at public community, junior, or technical colleges or private vocational and technical schools. In addition, you can take special courses offered by both the local and the national Associated Locksmiths of America. The national organization schedules classes in more than thirty subjects in its annual conventions. It can take anywhere from three months to four years to learn all the aspects of your craft.

Locksmiths work in many settings: small shops, large industrial firms, schools, hospitals, and government facilities.

The duties performed are the same for an employee and a self-employed locksmith. However, a self-employed locksmith must also be concerned with selling and making customer contacts. But both types of workers:

- repair damaged locks: disassemble lock and replace worn tumblers, springs, and other parts;
- install locks: determine type of lock needed; drill proper opening in selected location; fit lock in place, using hand and small power tools;
- make duplicate keys: using a rotary file, milling cutter, or tracing lathe, clamp key in place and guide tracing bar over original key, cutting the pattern into the duplicate key blank;
- rekey: change tumblers of a lock to fit a new key;
- open locks accidentally closed: release lock with lock picks, listening devices; drill and wrench the lock, destroying it if necessary;
- install or service electronic alarm and surveillance systems, including burglar alarms and access control systems.

Locksmiths use a wide variety of specialized and ordinary hand and power tools. Some of them are safe jig, files, screwdrivers, pliers, tweezers, wrenches, lock picks, keycutting machines, and electric drills.

Many locksmiths perform all types of service. Increasingly, however, they are specializing in one or more of these categories:

- residential security: repairing, rekeying, installing locks and alarms;
- commercial security: consulting on system requirements; providing controlled-access and master-key systems; installing and maintaining hardware; and routine servicing;
- automotive: originating keys to vehicles; unlocking locked vehicles; installing burglar alarms;
- burglar alarms and electronics: designing and installing systems used with mechanical security devices to provide maximum controlled entry;
- safes: selling, servicing, and combination changing; opening safes when the combination isn't known; opening safes that have been damaged or burglarized.

Regardless of the specialty in which you work, you can look forward to several advantages:

- Earnings: $11 an hour in the 1980s; wages vary with location and type of service; some sales work is paid on a commission basis.
- Hours: 5-day, 40-hour week; overtime for emergencies at night or on weekends;
- Fringe benefits: paid vacations and holidays; sick pay; health insurance.

Working in your repair shop, you'll usually be in a clean, well-equipped, and safe location. But you may have to drive to sites and work under greatly varying conditions. You should also consider some disadvantages in this occupation arising from tension and pressure caused by stress during emergencies as well as demands for quick service, and being on call at night and on weekends.

Women may find an additional burden in this predominantly male vocation: a reluctance to hire and train them. Although April Truitt's employer is very supportive of her, she says she has always felt it necessary to "do more" and accept more of the emergency overtime work, especially at the beginning of her career.

But Ms. Truitt says that her salary now is higher than those of most of her friends with college degrees who went into teaching or clerical jobs. Furthermore, she enjoys much satisfaction—particularly, she says, "when I open a safe after three others have failed. Women shouldn't allow themselves to be programmed. If you have a talent for mechanical work, go into it. You'll always be secure as a locksmith, and you won't be replaced by a computer."

Efforts to establish a career in this trade may be very worthwhile, since job openings for locksmiths with good skills will increase through the 1980s. Moreover, there'll be additional vacancies to replace workers who leave, retire, or change jobs. The outlook for locksmiths who are licensed to install and service electronic security systems is particularly favorable. Although trainees will find competition for jobs, experienced locksmiths will be very much in demand.

The security industry is seldom affected by economic ups and downs. Also, locksmiths are needed in every state, but most of all in places of growing population and industry.

Locksmiths can look forward to advancement in the form of salary raises rather than promotion, because most businesses are in small shops. However, locksmiths frequently go into business for themselves as another way to advance.

If you're a woman who enjoys mechanical work with varied and unusual duties, you'll find locksmithing particularly satisfying. Your skills will be needed throughout the country, enabling you to earn a good salary while gaining experience so that you can go into business for yourself.

For more information, contact:

- Associated Locksmiths of America, Inc.
  3003 Live Oak Street
  Dallas, TX 75204

MAINTENANCE ELECTRICIAN

Without a high school diploma or any special training, Teresa Calderon had few job options. The choices open to her were limited and similar to those she held as a typist, file clerk, and movie house usher, all low-paying, dead-end employment. But she applied to the Job Corps, a U.S. Department of Labor program, which arranged not only two-year training as an electrician's helper, but also an opportunity to earn a high school equivalency diploma. Because Teresa was in a residence program far from home, when she returned she sought help for job placement from a city agency that encouraged women to enter careers in nontraditional work. The agency found an opening for her as an apprentice maintenance electrician in a large hospital complex.

Today she's working in a planned program to learn one of the most highly skilled, respected, and well-paid crafts: that of electrician. Her trade is one that has steady employment, possibilities for advancement, and responsible, challenging duties.

If you're a woman between the ages of 16 of 21 years and are interested in a free program to learn a skilled trade, you can investigate the Job Corps. However, another requirement besides the age is that the applicant and her family be considered economically disadvantaged. You can ask a counselor at Job Corps for more specific information. Look in the telephone white pages under U.S. Government, Labor Department, to find the office nearest you.

On her new job Ms. Calderon found that one difference between maintenance and construction electricians is where and when they work; yet both need the same intensive, careful training. The maintenance electrician mainly does preventive and repair work on electrical systems already in place. The construction electrician installs those systems in buildings under construction.

Maintenance electricians work in factories, hospitals, hotels, apartment houses, and office buildings.

Even before considering job training, you should be aware of qualities the maintenance electrician needs:

- good health: there is lifting of heavy equipment; bending, stooping, and crouching in awkward positions; walking and standing for long periods of time;
- vision: good color discrimination is needed to identify colored wires; normal vision also is a requirement;
- manual dexterity and mechanical aptitude: you'd be manipulating and twisting wires, as well as using hand and power tools;
- personality: the capacity and desire to learn new skills as well as willingness to assume responsibility for your work; important also are patience and ability to get along with people.

There are several ways you could explore your interest in this occupation before investing in any intensive training:

- find summer employment as a helper to an electrician: apply directly to electrical contracting firms by looking them up in the yellow pages under Electric Contractors; also check with the state employment service and help-wanted ads in newspapers;
- take high school courses in math, physics, and electricity and electronic shop;
- take vocational or technical school subjects such as blueprint reading and mechanical drawing;
- enroll in a women's outreach center for training in the use of hand tools or repair of electrical devices; the YWCA can direct you to a center near you.

Should you decide you want to become a maintenance electrician, the most recommended way to do so is by a formal apprenticeship. You need to be at least 18 years of age and a high school graduate. You'll be working under a specific arrangement supervised and planned by a joint committee of the International Brotherhood of Electrical Workers and the National Electrical Contractors. Information on how to obtain an apprenticeship can be obtained from:

- The Bureau of Apprenticeship Training: look under U.S. Government, Labor Department, in the telephone white pages for the nearest office;
- Apprenticeship Council of the State Department of Labor: check the telephone white pages under your state government listings;
- International Brotherhood of Electrical Workers: find the local office in the yellow pages under Labor Organizations.
- state employment service;
- National Joint Apprenticeship and Training Committee for the Electrical Industry, 9700 East George Palmer Highway, Lanham, MD 20706.

Applicants for an apprenticeship are evaluated by a committee composed of union members and employer representatives as to education, experience, physical status, and references.

If an applicant passes the evaluation, she is enrolled in a four-year on-the-job training program supplemented by 144 hours of classes each year. Her pay begins at 50 percent of an experienced electrician's salary, with regular raises.

Classroom subjects include:

- electrical code requirements,
- safety and first-aid practices,
- blueprint reading,
- electrical theory,
- electronics,
- mathematics,
- drafting.

As an apprentice, some of the techniques she learns are:

- drilling holes;

- setting anchors;
- setting up conduits;
- measuring, bending, and installing conduits;
- installing, connecting, and testing wiring;
- setting up and drawing diagrams for entire electrical systems;
- welding, brazing, and burning.

Another route for entering this trade is the one that Teresa Calderon followed. You can take your craft theory and laboratory courses in a special facility such as the Job Corps or in:

- public community, technical, or junior college;
- private vocational, trade, or technical school; write for information to National Association of Trade and Technical Schools, 2251 Wisconsin Avenue, NW, Washington, DC 20007.
- Women's Bureau, U.S. Department of Labor; this agency may provide you with information about special training resources for women; look in the telephone white pages for the office nearest you.

Graduates of these schools can work in an informal, planned, on-the-job training situation until all aspects of the trade are covered and the trainee achieves journeyperson status. It usually takes about two years.

It's also possible to become a maintenance electrician through unplanned, on-the-job training as a helper to an employer. However, in such a situation you have no assurance that you'll get training in all the phases of the work necessary to qualify as a skilled maintenance electrician.

Trainees and apprentices must know not only the National Electric Code, but also city and state electric and building codes. In some localities electricians must be licensed.

After completing an apprenticeship or an on-the-job training program, a maintenance electrician may specialize by working on particular electrical equipment, or for manufacturing, commercial, or public institutions. Regardless of the industry or location, most of her duties are concerned with preventive maintenance along with repair work. A few of the tasks of these electricians are to:

- periodically inspect and test electrical equipment and wiring;
- clean and lubricate machinery parts as necessary;
- replace defective wiring, fuses, or small parts on motors, transformers, and switchboards;
- repair switches and other electrical equipment and fixtures;
- dismantle electrical equipment; replace or repair defective parts;
- reassemble the equipment, test it, and remount it;
- install new electrical equipment following oral instructions or blueprints, drawings, or layouts.

In performing their work electricians use a variety of hand tools such as screwdrivers, pliers, knives, wrenches, hacksaws, and drills.

In addition they use power tools and testing equipment such as pipe threaders, conduit benders, ammeters, oscilloscopes, and voltmeters.

On the job the journeyperson maintenance electrician often works without supervision. She must have a strong sense of responsibility, because careless work can result in burns or fires. But work done well offers not only satisfaction and feelings of pride and accomplishment, but excellent benefits:

- Wages: $16 to $25 per hour, depending on union membership, industry, and area; overtime and holiday pay are also governed by contract.
- Hours: 32- to 40-hour workweek; in industries operating on a 24-hour schedule, the maintenance electrician may work on any of the three 8-hour shifts.
- Paid vacations and holidays, usually part of the union contract, vary according to location and industry.
- Fringe benefits: retirement plans, health and life insurance, paid sick leave.
- Steady employment: jobs are not subject to seasonal fluctuations as in the case of construction electricians.

Though maintenance electricians usually work in a finished building, their environment can vary from clean, air-conditioned offices to dirty, noisy factory areas. In addition, there may be other disadvantages:

- hazards from electrical shocks and burns; good safety procedures lessen these dangers;
- injuries and cuts from tools and other sharp objects;
- risks from falls off ladders or scaffolds.

Being the only woman in the electrician's department can be lonely, notes Teresa Calderon. She says that the men are distant and "stiff." She feels strongly that this is an excellent trade and very suitable for women, but she advises that you'll need patience and self-control to eventually feel more comfortable with your male co-workers.

Efforts to overcome the sense of isolation some women feel in nontraditional work settings have led them to form or join groups that offer support and encouragement. You may be able to find out about such an organization from:

- YWCA
- National Organization for Women
- Women's Bureau, U.S. Department of Labor
- state employment service

One of the most promising aspects of the electrician's field is the future outlook for jobs. The total number of new job openings is among the highest of all craft occupations and will continue to be so through the 1990s. That means that with proper training and experience you can look forward to finding work without too much trouble.

With additional experience and seniority, a maintenance electrician can look forward to these promotion possibilities:

- supervisor,
- crew chief,
- head of maintenance department,
- independent electrical contractor,
- instructor in trade or vocational school,
- estimator for contractor,
- sales representative for building-supply contractor,
- electrical inspector.

The union that a maintenance electrician belongs to depends on the industry or business in which she is employed. Some of them are

- International Union of Electrical, Radio and Machine Workers
- International Association of Machinists and Aerospace Workers
- United Steelworkers of America

In the event that you enter the high-paying trade of maintenance electrician, you'll be doing work that is seldom routine, often varied, and needed throughout the country.

For more information, contact:

- Independent Electrical Contractors, Inc.
  1101 Connecticut Avenue, NW
  Washington, DC 20036
- International Brotherhood of Electrical Workers
  1125 15th Street, NW
  Washington, DC 20005
- National Electrical Contractors Association
  7315 Wisconsin Avenue
  Bethesda, MD 20814
- Associated Builders and Contractors
  729 15th Street, NW
  Washington, DC 20005

Chapter VII

Summary

Today's American woman has the choice of many exciting nontraditional jobs to fulfill her talents and abilities. After deciding what career you'd like, the next big step is getting that special job, the one offering a good salary, interesting challenges, and opportunities for advancement. Finding employment requires planning for:

- locating the position,
- filling out an application,
- participating in an interview.

In this chapter, you'll learn about some methods that will help you with these important stages.

The first item you need, even before beginning the job hunt, is a social security number. If you don't have one, apply for it at the Social Security Administration. You'll find the office nearest you in the telephone white pages under Social Security Administration.

Second, since most employers want some routine factual information about you, it is helpful to prepare your own fact sheet. On this sheet, or card, you can list the data you usually need. Then you can carry it with you, so that you'll always be prepared for the same requests.

On your sheet or card, list your schools and dates of graduation going back to the eighth grade. Record any courses, the dates completed, and the school where taken that apply to the job in which you're interested. Prior work history means your previous jobs, and most employers want to know some details about your work history. You'll need to list the names and addresses of your past employers and the dates of employment, even if the positions were part time or temporary. Always give your most recent jobs first. For references, list three people who can give information as to your reliability, character, and work habits. Teachers, counselors, and past or present employers are good choices. Be sure to ask these people in advance if you may use them as references. Also—since some employers ask—make a note of your mother's maiden name.

Having your fact sheet with you when you're filling out applications makes the task easier. You'll be able to concentrate on working neatly, and you'll avoid spelling errors by having the correct material already on paper. Be sure to take a pen when you're applying for a job; one with erasable ink is good insurance against sloppy, scratched-out forms.

Every community has resources for finding jobs, including women's centers such as those operated by the YWCA or other private groups. Many of them have obtained grants for vocational training and employment referral. These centers emphasize nontraditional jobs for women, and almost all have referral services. Check to see if you are near such a center, and apply there for help.

Unions and trade and professional organizations have information about obtaining jobs in their particular industry. Many maintain job banks for women and other minority groups. You can find the addresses and telephone numbers of specific organizations in the telephone yellow pages under Labor Organizations or Associations.

Another excellent way of getting a nontraditional job is through the recommendation of people you know, especially parents, relatives, and friends. This has always been a valuable entry route into a trade. If you don't have such a close connection, ask neighbors, teachers, and schoolmates if they know anyone who can help you get the job you want. Let as many people as possible know that you're looking for work.

In addition to personal contacts, explore the possibilities of your school guidance or placement office. They may have some specific jobs or suggestions for applying for a job-training program.

An important source of jobs in every community is the state employment department. The department may have different divisions such as Apprenticeship and Training, but all states have employment services. Your state agency is free and has a large bank of jobs. The counselors there can refer you to nontraditional job opportunities. Branches are located in most large cities and many smaller towns. You can find your local branch in the telephone white pages under State Services.

Help-wanted ads in the classified section of the newspaper can also furnish job leads. These ads are generally brief and require follow-up by letter or telephone call. Another way to search for a job is to visit a factory, shop, or personnel office of a business and inquire about openings. If you're in an industrial area, be alert for help-wanted signs outside buildings.

Whether you reach a personnel office, a state employment agency, or a union apprenticeship committee, you'll be asked to fill out an application. Occasionally, you'll be interviewed immediately, but usually you'll be given an appointment for the personal interview. Always be on time for this important meeting, and go alone! Don't take a friend for moral support. Learn the travel route beforehand, and time yourself to arrive ten minutes early. That way you can tell the receptionist who you are and whom you wish to see. The clothing you wear for this interview is important; it should be businesslike and adapted to the site and the type of position you're seeking. For example, if you're applying for a job in a machine shop, garage, or construction site, a clean blouse and pressed pants are appropriate. Keep your hair style and makeup simple. Jewelry should be be kept to a minimum. During the interview speak clearly and look at the interviewer. Don't whisper, mumble, or look away. If you ordinarily chew gum or smoke, don't do so for the interview.

Be prepared to tell what you have to offer for this specific job in training or experience. Don't hesitate to show enthusiasm and interest; by doing so, you can sometimes overcome the handicap of incomplete qualifications. Answer questions honestly, briefly, and without hesitating.

Finally, when the interview is over, thank the interviewer. If the employer doesn't definitely offer you the job or tell you when you'll hear about it, ask when you may call to learn the decision. Should you learn that you won't get the job, ask to have your application kept in the active file so that you may be considered for future openings.

Landing that special job may take time and persistence. You may also have to try several different approaches and even reapply to the same company every two or three months. Even if you take a job that's not quite the one you wanted in a particular industry, you can make contacts and be alerted for the opening you want. While waiting, you can sharpen your skills by taking courses in a trade school, an evening vocational school, or an outreach or women's center program. Your goals are important, and you should pursue them with determination and resolution.

Chapter VIII

Writing Yourself Up

RÉSUMÉ

A résumé is a fact sheet giving data about you and your job qualifications. It is similar to an application because it includes your name, address, education, experience, affiliations (job-related organizations), and references. Your résumé should be typed on one sheet of white paper with one-inch margins all around. You need to be brief and concise. These are the major parts of your résumé:

- Address: place your name, address, and telephone number at the top of the page; don't use abbreviations.
- Personal data: it is illegal for an employer to consider factors such as marital status, age, or health in the hiring process; however, if you feel that giving this information may be advantageous to you for the job you want, it is all right to do so.
- Education: describe your most recent training first; give only courses that apply to the job you want.
- Experience: list your employment starting with your most recent job; include your title, the company's name and address, and the dates you worked.
- Affiliations: give only job-related organizations.
- References: list two or three people with their names and addresses.

SAMPLE RÉSUMÉ

Tina Wise
6572 Lake Drive
Pines Lakes, Michigan 80072
(612) 922-7010

Personal Data
Date of Birth: 8/1/60
Marital Status: Single
Health: Excellent

Education
1985: *Associated Locksmiths of Michigan*. Workshop in Electronic Security System Installation
1984: *Pine Lakes Community College*: Business Management
1978–1983: Pine Lakes High School (graduate)

Employment
1983–Present: Locksmith, *Ajax Locks*, 211 Maple Street, Pine Valley, Michigan. Major duties: repairing, rekeying, and installing residential and commercial locks; unlocking vehicles, installing vehicle antitheft devices
1978–1982: Stock clerk, *Main Street Hardware*, 23 Main
(summers) Street, Fort Pines, Michigan

Affiliations
Associated Locksmiths of Michigan

References
Mr. J. Watkins, Manager
Ajax Locksmiths
211 Maple Street
Pine Valley, Michigan

Dr. Thomas Smith
Pine Lakes Community College
Pine Lakes, Michigan

Mr. Sammuel Trevor, Manager
Main Street Hardware
23 Main Street
Fort Pines, Michigan

LETTER OF APPLICATION

No matter what kind of work you do, your letter of application is important. Since it will be sent along with your résumé, one sheet for this type of letter is sufficient. If possible, address your letter to a specific person; include this information:

- State the name of the particular job you're applying for.
- Give a reason you think you can do this job.
- Request an interview.
- Include telephone number where you can be reached.

Sample Letter of Application

>   6572 Lake Drive
>   Pine Lakes, MI 80072
>   January 15, 1987

Mr. Bradley Johnson
CTF Industries, Inc.
Harding Boulevard
Fayetville, MI 80071

Dear Mr. Johnson:

Please consider my application for the experienced locksmith's job as advertised in the *Fayetville Daily News* on January 14, 1987.

For the past four years I've been employed as a locksmith and worked on commercial, residential, and automobile locks in a wide range of duties. In addition, I've taken training in electronic security systems and business management. You will find the details of my qualifications in my enclosed résumé.

May I have a personal interview to discuss this position with you? I can be reached at (612) 934-2211 from 8:00 a.m. to 4:00 p.m, or at (612) 922-7010 after 5:00 p.m.

>   Sincerely yours,

"THANK YOU" LETTER

Sending a "thank you" letter on the same day or the day after a job interview is a courtesy not many applicants observe. However, such a brief, handwritten note may make you stand out among other job seekers with similar qualifications. You can use this simple outline:

Dear Mr. Johnson:

Thank you for talking to me yesterday about the locksmith vacancy in your company. The job sounds very interesting and I feel my four years' experience, combined with my additional training, make me well qualified for the position. Since you gave me a very good idea of what would be expected, I'm more enthusiastic than ever, and confident that I can be an asset to your firm.

I'll call in a few days, and hope you will have reached a favorable decision about my application.

                                              Sincerely yours,

Chapter **XI**

The Twenty-first Century: Women's Workforce

At the edge of the twenty-first century, you as a working woman will be at the center of changes that will produce an America vastly different from the one we know today. While today's jobs and skills will earn you today's pay, will your job still exist beyond the year 2000? If it does, will it be in the same form, and will your skills be adequate to earn enough to cover tomorrow's needs?

We expect several important trends to shape the coming century. If you're aware of them you'll be much better equipped to plan for your own future. We expect that:

- Service industries will create most new jobs.
- The labor force will contain many more women, older workers, and disadvantaged persons.
- Workers in the service areas will need more expertise and knowledge for the new, more demanding jobs.
- Manufacturing industries will decline and be a much smaller part of our economy.

Now more than ever you need to anticipate questions about what fields offer you advantages such as many openings, high pay, and likely promotions. The answers may be in one of the key changes predicted for the United States—the growth of service industries. Those are:

- Finance, insurance, real estate.
- Public administration: federal, state, and local government.

- Wholesale and retail trade.
- Transportation, communication, public utilities.
- Health, education.

In all the above areas, three broad occupation groups will be in the greatest demand:

- Technicians such as computer technician, business machine repairer.
- Executives and managers.
- Professionals such as doctors, engineers, accountants.

Manufacturing industries making goods such as automobiles, clothing, and furniture will shrink. Therefore, you will see very few jobs for assemblers, machine operators, and laborers.

Some other important factors for working women by 2000 and beyond:

- An increase of women in the total work force; about 47 percent, or just under half of the total, will be women.
- Many more women will be working, even those with young children; 6 out of 7 working-age women will hold jobs.
- Older women will be staying longer in the labor force; the average ages of working women will be between 35 and 54 years.

Because today's customs covering pay scales, maternity leaves, pensions, welfare, and other benefits were designed for a time when men were the breadwinners and women the homemakers, look for changes in those policies. In the twenty-first century American society will be one in which everyone is expected to work. Some important responses to these conditions, of special interest to women, will be:

- Increased quality day care for children.
- Convenience food products and more home delivery.
- More time off for pregnancy leave and child-rearing duties.

Moreover, the workplace will be restructured to allow a woman to accommodate both her job and her family life. New, creative uses in the duration of the job will allow women to participate fully in the workplace. Also, this new diversity will give women additional time and resources for their children. Predictions for alternative work patterns include:

- Flexitime: employees may vary daily, weekly, or yearly work schedules.
- Compressed work schedule: a full-time employee could work the hourly equivalent of a 5-day week in either a 4- or 3-day week.
- Job sharing: one full-time job is accomplished by two or more persons, each working part time.
- Part-time work: convenient for workers who need to supplement income, keep up skills, or gain work experience.
- Temporary work: for retraining or as a stopgap before permanent employment, or for first-time entrants to a job.

In addition to more flexible approaches to hours, another employment prospect will be the increased level of expertise or knowledge needed to hold a job. By the twenty-first century, the majority of all new positions will require post-high school training and education. For the immediate future, there has never been a better time for a woman to invest in job counseling, education, and training. By doing so she will be able to share in the benefits of job security, higher salaries, and promotional opportunities of the sophisticated new jobs on the horizon. Since there will be very little employment for those who cannot read, follow directions, or use mathematics, women will need to:

- Go to school longer: post-high school training for one or more years.
- Study more difficult subjects and undertake a fuller program: math and science should be part of the curriculum.
- Pass more difficult tests: more time will have to be devoted to preparation and study.

Although your own personal needs and interests play the largest part in your decision about the occupation you want to pursue, you need to know what options will be in your future. Realistic and successful career planning must consider trends and demands in the employment forecast. If you are aware of the new developments you can consider them and match them with your own preferences.

While the future can't be predicted with complete certainty because of changes in the economy, government policies, and population trends, you can be ready for the job market of the twenty-first century. Here are some specific jobs that will be important by the year 2000 and beyond.

COMPUTER SERVICE TECHNICIAN

- Skills needed: mechanical aptitude; eye/hand coordination; patience; outgoing personality.
- Training: 1-2 years post-high school electronics or electrical training; on-the-job training and related classroom instruction as an apprentice on the job.
- Salary and hours: in the 1990's $500 to $740 per week; 35-40 hour weeks which may include shifts.
- Projected growth: much faster than the average for all occupations.
- Health and safety: some minor burns or electrical shock.

OFFICE/BUSINESS MACHINE REPAIRER

- Skills needed: mechanical aptitude; mathematical knowledge; eye/hand coordination; manual dexterity; neat appearance and outgoing personality.
- Training: post-high school one year; minimum training in electricity or electronics; additional special school training provided by manufacturers or independent repair shops; usually one to three years as apprentice before fully qualified.
- Salary and hours: in the 1990's $400 to $720 per week; 35-40 hours a week.
- Projected growth: faster than average for all occupations.
- Health and safety: No significant hazards.

RADIO AND TELEVISION SERVICE TECHNICIAN

- Skills needed: mechanical aptitude; eye/hand coordination; manual dexterity; attention to detail; outgoing personality.

- Training: post-high school training for 1 or 2 years; practical experience either in a formal or informal apprenticeship of 3 to 4 years; some states require a license exam.
- Salary and hours; in the 1990's $400 to $520 per week; hours are 35 to 40 hours per week with some evenings and weekends.
- Projected growth: about as fast as the average for all occupations.
- Health and safety: some hazards from electrical shock and strains from lifting and carrying heavy equipment.

FIREFIGHTER

- Skills needed: mechanical aptitude; physical strength; independent decision-making; good judgment; outgoing personality.
- Training: must be 18 years or over and a high school graduate; after passing written and physical tests, training by government agencies is offered for periods of several months; usually apprenticeship programs lasting 3 to 4 years.
- Salary and hours: in the 1990's average annual beginning salary about $22,000; hours are 35 to 40 hours per week but include shifts covering weekends, holidays, and all hours of the day and night.
- Projected growth: about as fast as the average for all occupations.
- Health and safety: involves risk and injury from fire and smoke as well as building cave-ins; contact with harmful gases and chemicals.

Appendix A
U.S. Agencies

Women's Bureau
U.S. Department of Labor
200 Constitution Avenue, NW
Washington, DC 20210

This agency serves and promotes the interests of working women and is concerned with women's employment, legal rights, and economic well-being. Local regional offices are:

Region I
Room 1700-C JFK Building
Boston, 02203
(Connecticut, Maine, Massachusetts, New Hampshire, Rhode Island, Vermont)

Region II
1515 Broadway
New York, NY 10036
(New Jersey, New York, Puerto Rico, Virgin Islands)

Region III
3535 Market Street
Philadelphia, PA 19104
(Delaware, District of Columbia, Maryland, Pennsylvania, Virginia, West Virginia)

Region IV
1371 Peachtree Street, NE
Atlanta, GA 30309
(Alabama, Florida, Georgia, Kentucky, Mississippi, North Carolina, South Carolina, Tennessee)

Region V
230 South Dearborn Street
Chicago, IL 60604
(Illinois, Indiana, Michigan, Minnesota, Ohio, Wisconsin)

Region VI
555 Griffin Square Building
Griffin and Young Streets
Dallas, TX 75202
(Arkansas, Louisiana, New Mexico, Oklahoma, Texas)

APPENDIX A

Region VII
2511 Federal Building
911 Walnut Street
Kansas City, MO 64106
(Iowa, Kansas, Missouri, Nebraska)

Region VIII
1432 Federal Building
1961 Stout Street
Denver, CO 80202
(Colorado, Montana, North Dakota, South Dakota, Utah, Wyoming)

Region IX
Room 11411, Federal Building
450 Golden Gate Avenue
San Francisco, CA 94102
(Arizona, California, Hawaii, Nevada)

Region X
Room 3032, Federal Office Building
909 First Avenue
Seattle, WA 98174
(Alaska, Idaho, Oregon, Washington)

Manpower Administration
U.S. Department of Labor
Washington, DC 20213

You can find the local address of this agency in the telephone white pages for information on training and employment in nontraditional work.

U.S. Bureau of Apprenticeship and Training
Patrick Henry Building
601 D Street, NW
Washington, DC 20213

Here are the regional offices of the BAT:

Region I
JFK Federal Bldg.
Room E-432
Boston, MA 02203
(Connecticut, New Hampshire, Maine, Rhode Island, Massachusetts, Vermont)

Region II
1515 Broadway
New York, NY 10036
(New Jersey, Puerto Rico, New York, Virgin Islands)

Region III
P.O. Box 8796
Philadelphia, PA 19101
(Delaware, Virginia, Maryland, West Virginia, Pennsylvania)

Region IV
1371 Peachtree Street, NE
Atlanta, GA 30367
(Albama, Mississippi, Florida, North Carolina, Georgia, South Carolina, Kentucky, Tennessee)

Region V
Federal Bldg.
230 South Dearborn Street
Chicago, IL 60604
(Illinois, Minnesota, Indiana, Ohio, Michigan, Wisconsin)

Region VI
555 Griffin Square Bldg.
Griffin and Young Sts.
Dallas, TX 75202
(Arkansas, Oklahoma, Louisiana, Texas, New Mexico)

Region VII
Federal Office Bldg.
911 Walnut Street
Kansas City, MO 64106
(Iowa, Missouri, Kansas, Nebraska)

Region VIII
U.S. Custom House
721 19th St.
Denver, CO 80202
(Colorado, South Dakota, Montana, Utah, North Dakota, Wyoming)

Region IX
211 Main Street
San Francisco, CA 94105-1978
Arizona, Hawaii, California, Nevada)

Region X
Federal Office Bldg.
909 First Avenue
Seattle, WA 98174
(Alaska, Oregon, Idaho, Washington)

These are the state offices of the BAT:

Alaska
Federal Building & Courthouse, Box 37
701 C Street
Anchorage 99513

Alabama
1931 9th Avenue, South
Birmingham 35205

Arizona
2120 North Central
Phoenix 85004

Arkansas
Federal Building
700 West Capitol Street
Little Rock 72201

California
211 Main Street
San Francisco 94105-1978

Colorado
U.S. Custom House
721 19th Street
Denver 80202

Connecticut
Federal Building
135 High Street
Hartford 06103

Delaware
Lock Box 36
Federal Bldg.
844 King Street
Wilmington 19801

APPENDIX A

Florida
227 North Bronough Street
Tallahassee 32301

Georgia
1371 Peachtree Street, NE
Atlanta 30367

Hawaii
P.O. Box 50203
300 Ala Moana Boulevard
Honolulu 95850

Idaho
1109 Main Street
Boise 83702

Illinois
7222 W. Cermak Road
North Riverside 60546

Indiana
46 E. Ohio Street
Indianapolis 46204

Iowa
210 Walnut Street
Des Moines 50309

Kansas
444 S.E. Quincy Street
Topeka 66683

Kentucky
600 Federal Place
Louisville 40202

Louisiana
8312 Florida Boulevard
Baton Rouge 70806

Maine
68 Sewall Street
Augusta 04330

Maryland
31 Hopkins Plaza
Baltimore 21201

Massachusetts
JFK Federal Building
Boston 02203

Michigan
300 East Michigan Avenue
Lansing 48933

Minnesota
316 Robert Street
St. Paul 55101

Mississippi
100 West Capitol Street
Jackson 39269

Missouri
210 North Tucker
St. Louis 63101

Montana
301 South Park Avenue
Helena 59626-0055

Nebraska
106 South 15th Street
Omaha 68102

Nevada
301 East Stewart Avenue
Las Vegas 89101

New Hampshire
55 Pleasant Street
Concord 03301

New Jersey
970 Broad Street
Newark 07102

New Mexico
505 Marquette NW
Albuquerque 87102

New York
512 U.S. Post Office
and Courthouse
Albany 12207

North Carolina
310 New Bern Avenue
Raleigh 27601

North Dakota
653 2nd Avenue, North
Fargo 58102

Ohio
200 North High Street
Columbus 43215

Oklahoma
50 Penn Place
Oklahoma City 73118

Oregon
1220 S.W. 3rd Avenue
Portland 97204

Pennsylvania
228 Walnut Street
Harrisburg 17108

Rhode Island
100 Hartford Avenue
Providence 02909

South Carolina
1835 Assembly Street
Columbia 29201

South Dakota
400 South Phillips Avenue
Sioux Falls 57102

Tennessee
1720 West End Avenue
Nashville 37203

Texas
2320 LaBranch Street
Houston 77004

Utah
350 South Main Street
Salt Lake City 84101

Vermont
96 College Street
Burlington 05401

Virginia
400 North 8th Street
Richmond 23240

Washington
1009 Federal Office Building
Seattle 98174

West Virginia
500 Quarrier Street
Charleston 25301

Wisconsin
212 E. Washington Avenue
Madison 53703

Wyoming
2120 Capitol Avenue
Cheyenne 82001

Appendix B
State Apprenticeship Agencies

Though the state agencies don't recruit or place apprentices, they may suggest resources such as other government agencies, union committees, or employer organizations that can help you.

Arizona
Apprenticeship Services
Department of Economic
  Security
207 East McDowell Road
Phoenix 85004

California
Division of Apprenticeship
  Standards
Department of Industrial
  Relations
455 Golden Gate Avenue,
San Francisco 94102

Colorado
Apprenticeship Council
Division of Labor
323 Centennial Building
Denver 80203

Connecticut
Apprentice Training Division
Department of Labor
200 Folly Brook Boulevard
Wethersfield 06109

Delaware
Apprenticeship Officer
Delaware State Department of
  Labor
820 North French Street
Wilmington 19801

District of Columbia
DC Apprenticeship Council
500 C Street, NW
Washington 20001

Florida
Bureau of Apprenticeship
Division of Labor
Department of Labor and
  Employment Security
1321 Executive Center Drive,
East Tallahassee 32301

Hawaii
Apprenticeship Division
Department of Labor and
  Industrial Relations
825 Mililani Street
Honolulu 96813

Kansas
Apprenticeship Section
Division of Labor-Management
 Relations and Employment
 Standards
Department of Human
 Resources
512 West 6th Street
Topeka 66603-3178

Kentucky
Apprenticeship and Training
Kentucky State Apprenticeship
 Council
620 South Third Street
Louisville 40202

Louisiana
Division of Apprenticeship
Department of Labor
P.O. Box 44094
Baton Rouge 70804

Maine
Maine State Apprenticeship
 and Training Council—
 Department of Manpower
 Affairs
Bureau of Labor
State Office Building
Augusta 04333

Maryland
Apprenticeship and Training
Maryland Apprenticeship and
 Training Council
Division of Labor and Industry
203 East Baltimore Street
Baltimore 21202

Massachusetts
Division of Apprentice Training
Department of Labor and
 Industries
100 Cambridge Street
Boston 02202

Minnesota
Division of Voluntary
 Apprenticeship
Department of Labor and
 Industry
444 Lafayette Road
St. Paul 55101

Montana
Apprenticeship Bureau
Division of Labor Standards
Department of Labor and
 Industry
Capitol Station
Helena 59620

Nevada
Department of Labor
505 East King Street
Carson City 89710

New Hampshire
Commission of Labor
Department of Labor
19 Pillsbury Street
Concord 03301

New Mexico
N.M. State Apprenticeship
 Council
Labor and Industrial Commiss
2340 Menaul, NE
Albuquerque 87107

APPENDIX B

New York
Apprentice Training
Department of Labor
The Campus Building, #12
Albany 12240

North Carolina
Apprenticeship Division
North Carolina Department of Labor
4 West Edenton Street
Raleigh 27601-1472

Ohio
State Apprenticeship Council
Department of Industrial Relations
2323 West Fifth Avenue
Columbus 43215

Oregon
Apprenticeship and Training Division
1400 SW Fifth Avenue
Portland 97201

Pennsylvania
Pennsylvania Apprenticeship and Training Council
Department of Labor & Industry
7th and Forster Streets
Harrisburg 17120

Puerto Rico
Apprenticeship Division
Department of Labor
Right to Employment Division
GPO Box 4452
San Juan 00936

Rhode Island
Apprenticeship Council
Department of Labor
220 Elmwood Avenue
Providence 02907

Utah
Apprenticeship Council
160 East 3rd South
Salt Lake City 84110

Vermont
Vermont Apprenticeship Council
Department of Labor and Industry
120 State Street
Montpelier 05602

Virgin Islands
Division of Apprenticeship and Training
Department of Labor
Christiansted, St. Croix 00820

Virginia
Division of Apprenticeship Training
Virginia Department of Labor and Industry
P.O. Box 12064
Richmond 20064

Washington
Apprenticeship and Training Division
Department of Labor and Industries
4436 Lacey Boulevard, SE
Lacey 98603

Wisconsin
Division of Apprenticeship and
 Training
Department of Industry, Labor
 and Human Relations
P.O. Box 7946
Madison 53707

Appendix C
Women's Organizations

These organizations operate national programs to recruit and prepare individuals for apprenticeships and other skilled blue-collar work. Several have special programs for women. You can write to them to find a program near you:

Young Women's Christian Association
600 Lexington Avenue
New York, NY 10022

National Urban League
Labor Education Advancement Program (LEAP)
500 East 62nd Street
New York, NY 10021
   Recruits and places minorities and women in skilled jobs and apprenticeships through LEAP programs in cities across the country.

Human Resources Development Institute (HRDI)
AFL-CIO
815 16th Street, NW
Washington, DC 20006
   The employment and training arm of the AFL-CIO that operates apprenticeship outreach programs for minorities and women. Programs are sponsored by local building trades councils.

Minority Women Employment Program
148 International Building
Atlanta, GA 30303
   Operates employment, counseling, and placement programs for women.

Opportunities Industrialization
Centers of America (OIC's)
Broad and Thompson Streets
Philadelphia, PA 19121
    OIC's operate in many cities to provide programs to motivate, train, and place community residents in manufacturing and industrial jobs.

Recruitment and Training Program (R-T-P), Inc.
162 Fifth Avenue
New York, NY 10010
    Operates local outreach and placement programs for minorities and women in skilled nontraditional jobs and apprenticeships.

SER—Jobs for Progress, Inc.
(Service-Employment Redevelopment)
9841 Airport Boulevard
Los Angeles, CA 90045
    Offers outreach, training, counseling, and job-hunting skills training for minorities and women, particularly for Hispanics, through local SER projects.

Wider Opportunities for Women (WOW)
1511 K Street, NW
Washington, DC 20005
    Offers information, advice, and training resources for nontraditional jobs.

International Union of Electrical, Radio and Machine Workers (AFL-CIO)
Education & Women's Activities
1126 16th Street, NW
Washington, DC 20036
    Offers job training in electronics, electrical, and allied industries.

National Association of Women in Construction
2800 West Lancester
Ft. Worth, TX 76107
    Although this group is mainly for management women, it also offers scholarships and educational programs.

APPENDIX C

Some of these groups have local chapters. You can find them in the telephone white pages or write to the national offices to find a chapter near you. They offer information about local resources for training for nontraditional jobs.

National Organization for Women (NOW)
425 13th Street, NW
Washington, DC 20004

Coalition of Labor Union Women
8731 East Jefferson
Detroit, MI 48214

National Congress of Neighborhood Women
690 Metropolitan Avenue
Brooklyn, NY 11211

National Women's Trucking Association
40 Pendleton Street
Charleston, SC 29403

Union Women's Alliance to Gain Equality (Union WAGE)
P.O. Box 462
Berkeley, CA 94701

Displaced Homemakers Network
National Headquarters
1010 Vermont Avenue, NW
Washington DC 20005

Women in Self Help (WISH)
421 Fifth Avenue
Brooklyn, NY 11215

This organization is primarily for women living in the New York City area, but has information on similar groups around the country.

If you belong to a minority or ethnic group, one of the organizations below may be able to help you find training and a job in nontraditional work. Write to find a branch near you.

North American Indian
  Women's Association
720 Spruce Street NW
Siseton, SD 57262

Americans for Indian
  Opportunity
600 2nd Street
Albuquerque, NM 87102

Council of Asian Pacific
  Organizations
Los Angeles, CA 90017

Japanese American Citizens'
  League
1765 Sutter Street
San Francisco, CA 94115

Organization of Chinese
  American Women
3214 Quesada Street, NW
Washington, DC 20015

Chinese for Affirmative Action
669 Clay Street
San Francisco, CA 94111

National Council of Negro
  Women
1346 Connecticut Avenue, NW
Washington, DC 20036

Black Women's Employment
  Project
NAACP Legal Defense and
  Education Fund, Inc.
10 Columbus Circle
New York, NY 10019

Black Women Organized for
  Action
P.O. Box 15072
San Francisco, CA 94115

National Chicana Foundation
2114 Commerce
San Antonio, TX 78207

ASPIRA of America, Inc.
245 Fifth Avenue
New York, NY 10016

National Council of La Raza
1025 15th Street NW
Washington, DC 20005

American G.I. Forum
Women's Programs
5475 Yale Drive
San Jose, CA 95118

National Conference of Puerto
  Rican Women
P.O. Box 4804
Cleveland Park Station
Washington, DC 20008

National Association for Puerto
  Rican Civil Rights
175 East 116th Street
New York, NY 10029

National Council of Jewish
  Women
15 East 26th Street
New York, NY 10010

B'nai B'rith Career Counseling
  Service
1640 Rhode Island Avenue NW
Washington, DC 20036

Index

A

accuracy, 17, 20, 33, 39, 77, 85, 107, 114
advancement, opportunities for, 10-11, 15, 20, 25, 30, 32, 36, 42, 45, 48, 55, 62, 68, 74, 82, 88, 95, 96, 98, 105, 111, 117-118, 123
affirmative action, 27, 89
airconditioning refrigeration and heating mechanic, 76-82
aircraft mechanic, 83-89
American Women in Radio and Television, 62
ammeter, 122
application, job, 125, 127, 131
apprenticeship, 2, 6, 11, 46, 77, 91, 114
  formal, 7, 13, 17, 23, 79, 93-94, 119-120
  informal, 8, 13, 22
aptitude, mechanical, 6, 11, 27, 31, 33, 35, 36, 39, 43, 45, 77, 79, 85, 96, 107, 119
attitudes, co-workers', 3, 5, 10, 19, 24, 30, 36, 42, 49, 55, 68, 75, 81, 88, 93, 111, 117, 123
audio
  control technician, 56
  engineer, 54
auto mechanic, 3, 89-95, 114

B

benefits, fringe, 6, 10, 15, 30, 32, 35, 36, 41, 47, 54, 61, 67, 68, 71, 74, 81, 87, 96, 98, 104, 111, 117, 122, 134
Billings, Bonnie, 69-70, 74, 75
Bliss, Oceania, 20, 22
blueprint reading, 7, 8, 13, 17, 28, 39, 45, 46, 79, 114, 119
boiler tender, 95-99
bonding, 115
broadcast technician, 49-56
building custodian, 99-105
Bureau of Apprenticeship, 7, 13, 17, 79, 120
bus driver, 63-69
Butler, Renee, 49, 55

C

cable splicer, 3, 26-31, 37, 40, 41, 46
Calderon, Teresa, 118-119, 121, 123
camera operator, 56-62
carpenter, 3, 6-11
central office technician, 32-37
Clark, Esther, 89
college, community, 8, 51, 58, 61, 78, 99, 103, 115, 121
color
  perception, 39, 45, 51, 58, 77, 85, 107, 119
  sense of, 22
communication industry, 134
communication skills, 58, 107
computer, 91, 105, 110
concentration, power of, 51, 58
construction industry, 5-25
coordination, eye-hand, 45, 58, 64, 77, 114
crafts, skilled, 2, 5, 32, 43
creativity, 58
Crosby, Arlene, 105-106, 111
customer service, 26

D

Davis, Betty, 26
day care, 134
depth perception, 64, 114
dexterity, manual, 6, 11, 15, 17, 22, 27, 31, 33, 35, 36, 39, 43, 45, 51, 77, 79, 85, 96, 107, 114, 119
drawing, mechanical, 7, 17, 28, 33, 39, 45, 77, 83, 108, 114, 119
driver education, 64
driver-sales worker, 72, 73, 74
driving, 117
  defense, 65
  enjoying, 63, 68, 69
  record, 72, 115
dynamometer, 91

E

education, 134
electrician, 3, 118-124
electric power industry, 26-31
electronic new gathering (ENG), 56, 60
electronics technician, 3, 105-112
emergency duty, 29, 30, 36, 39, 41, 47, 55, 61, 68, 114, 117
employer, 2-3, 5, 7, 13, 67, 79, 120

151

employment service, state, 126-127
examination
  licensing, 54, 85, 97
  physical, 8, 64, 65, 69, 71
executives, 134

F
fact sheet, personal, 125-126
Federal Aviation Administration (FAA), 83, 85, 88
Federal Communications Commission (FCC), 54
finance, 133
financial air, 51, 59, 108
firefighter, 137
flexitime, 135
foods, convenience, 134
frame wirer, 33, 34

G
glazier, 3, 16-20

H
harassment, on-the-job, 3, 5, 10, 13, 19, 24, 30, 42, 61
health, good, 16, 22, 23, 31, 33, 37, 42, 64, 65, 71, 77, 94, 105, 115, 119, 134
Holmes, Sharon, 16, 17, 19
hours of work
  computer service technician, 136
  construction, 19, 25
  electric power, 30
  firefighter, 137
  mechanics/repairers, 81, 87, 98, 104, 111, 117, 122, 136, 137
  telephone, 35, 41, 47
  television, 54, 61
  transportation, 67, 74

I
insurance, 133
internship, television, 49
interview, job, 6, 8, 11, 125, 127

J
Job Corps, 118-119, 121
job-finding resources, 126-127
job outlook
  construction, 5, 10, 15, 19, 25
  electric power, 26, 30
  mechanics/repairers, 76, 82, 88, 95, 98, 105, 112, 117, 123
  telephone, 32, 36, 42, 47
  television, 49, 55, 62
  transportation, 63, 68, 74
joint committee, apprenticeship, 2, 6, 7-8, 13, 18, 23, 79, 94, 120

L
Lane, Maryann, 6, 10
Layman, Eileen, 56, 60
layoffs, 5, 26, 30, 35, 41, 68, 81, 88
letter
  application, 131
  "thank you," 132
license
  airframe, 83, 85
  boiler tender, 97
  chauffeur, 64, 71
  driver, 64
  electrician, 121
  FAA, 88
  FCC, 61
  locksmith, 117
  powerplant, 83, 85
  radiotelephone operator, 54
line installer, telephone, 37-43, 46
locksmith, 3, 112-118
Lun, Laverne, 99-100

M
maintenance electrician, 118-124
manager, 134
manufacturing industry, 134
manometer, 81
maternity leave, 134
math, 4, 7, 8, 13, 17, 39, 45, 51, 58, 77, 83, 94, 96, 107, 108, 112, 114, 119
Mathews, Mary Ellen, 43, 46
Matos, Sandra, 83
mechanics/repairers, 76, 123
microphone boom operator, 54

N
National Organization for Women (NOW), 4, 14, 20, 25, 30, 42, 98, 105, 123

O
ohmmeter, 46
  volt-, 81
oscilloscope, 46, 91, 110, 122
outreach women's, 6, 7, 17, 20, 25, 28, 33, 39, 42, 45, 76, 77, 83, 89, 94, 96, 102, 108, 114, 119, 128

P
painter, 20-25, 99
paperhanging, 24, 99
patience, 17, 20, 42, 114, 123
PBX installer, 46
physics, 33, 39, 45, 58, 77, 83, 108, 119
Piesco, Eileen, 32, 36
Poni-Baptiste, Arlene, 11
powerplant, 26, 83, 85
pressure, 68, 81, 87, 88, 117

INDEX 153

calmness under, 71
deadline, 51, 56, 61
public, dealing with, 45, 63, 68, 82, 102, 115, 119
public utilities, 134

R
real estate, 133
references, personal, 126
repair, electrical, 33, 39, 45, 83-84, 99, 108, 119
repair, office/business machine, 136
responsibility, 45, 63, 66, 71, 77, 85, 107, 119, 122
résumé, 129-131

S
safety practices, 10, 15, 19, 25, 28-29, 35, 42, 46, 47, 79, 81, 93, 98, 123
scholarship, 51, 108
school
  correspondence, 99, 115
  FAA-approved, 83, 85
  trade/vocational, 7, 8, 22, 28, 33, 39, 45, 46, 51, 58, 61, 71, 77, 78, 94, 96, 99, 103, 108, 114, 115, 119, 121, 128
science, courses in, 4, 51, 94, 107, 112
self-discipline, 35
service industries, 133-137
Shiffrin, Alice, 63, 66, 67, 68
shift work, 35, 41, 47, 54, 56, 61, 64, 67, 96, 98, 104, 111, 122, 136, 137
shop, courses in, 4, 17, 45, 51, 94, 108, 114
  electric, 28, 33, 83, 119
  machine, 39
  metal, 77, 83, 96, 102, 114
  wood, 7, 77, 96, 102, 114
social security number, 125
stamina, physical, 6, 10, 27, 37, 45, 58, 85
station
  cable TV, 55
  educational TV, 49, 52, 54
  radio, 49
  small, 55, 59
  television, 49, 53, 54, 56
stereotyping, sex, 3
stonemason, 3, 11-16
strength, physical, 22, 77, 85, 94, 115, 119
supervision, working without, 24, 35, 37, 43, 45, 67, 68, 69, 77, 102, 107, 115, 122
support group, women's, 14, 20, 43, 55, 62, 98, 104-105, 123

T
team, working as, 35, 36, 37, 56, 84
technician, 134
  computer service, 136
  radio/television service, 136-137
telephone industry, 3, 32-48
television industry, 49-62
tension, 55, 61, 68, 81, 88, 117
test
  apprenticeship, 79
  aptitude, 6, 8, 33, 40, 45, 96
  driving, 64, 69, 71
  written, 64, 65, 71
Thompson, Avis, 76-77, 81
tools
  care of, 8, 79
  hand, 6, 9, 14, 19, 33, 34, 39, 41, 45, 80, 87, 91-92, 104, 110, 116, 122
  owning, 24, 77, 92
  power, 6, 9, 14, 19, 28, 40, 41, 80, 87, 91-92, 104, 116, 122
  small, 33, 45
  working with, 4, 6, 13, 16, 17, 23, 28, 33, 83, 96, 101, 114, 119
trade, wholesale/retail, 134
training
  classroom, 8, 13, 18, 23, 32, 34, 36, 40, 46, 65, 72, 79, 94, 120
  continuing, 45, 47, 48, 58, 62, 81, 99, 111
  driver, 65, 71, 72
  on-the-job, 3, 5, 8, 11, 16, 17, 22, 26, 28, 32, 34, 36, 40, 46, 49, 53, 65, 77, 78, 91, 94, 96, 114, 120, 121
  post-high school, 2, 51, 102, 135, 136, 137
transit, local/intercity, 63, 66, 68
transmission/distribution, 26, 27
transmitter engineer, 54
transportation industry, 63-75, 134
truck driver, local, 69-75
Truitt, April, 112-114, 117

U
union, 3, 5, 6, 7, 13, 26, 67, 71, 74, 79, 88, 103, 111, 120, 122, 123, 126

V
video engineer, 53
voltmeter, 110, 122

W
wages
  construction, 5, 10, 15, 19, 25
  electric power, 29
  mechanics/repairers, 81, 87, 94, 95, 96, 97, 104, 111, 117, 120, 122
  telephone, 35, 41, 47
  television, 54, 61
  transportation, 67, 68, 69, 74
Welsh, Doris, 95-96, 98
Women in Broadcasting, 55
Women's Bureau, 4, 13, 15, 77, 98, 105, 121, 123
women's workforce, 133-137

Wood, Kathy, 37, 42
work history, 125
workers, service, 133-137
working conditions
  dirt, 4, 11, 81, 89, 93, 96, 98, 122
  extreme weather, 10, 15, 39, 42, 47, 55, 61, 74, 87, 93
  hazards, 10, 15, 19, 25, 29, 42, 47, 61, 68, 74, 81, 87, 93, 98, 104, 111, 117, 122, 136, 137
  heights, 4, 5, 6, 15, 19, 81
  indoor, 19, 32, 35, 54, 87, 98, 111, 117, 122
  noise, 4, 11, 36, 81, 87, 93, 98, 122
  outdoor, 4, 5, 6, 10, 11, 15, 27, 31, 37, 42-43, 47, 55, 61, 68, 69, 74
work schedules, altered, 135

Y
YWCA, 4, 6, 15, 20, 25, 28, 30, 33, 39, 42, 45, 77, 89, 96, 98, 102, 105, 108, 114, 119, 123, 126

16061

331.7
NEU
　Neufeld, Rose
　　Exploring nontraditional
　jobs for women
　　　　　　　　　　$11.40

DATE DUE

St. Mary Regional High School
Library
310 Augusta Street
South Amboy, New Jersey 08879